TOURISM AND TREKKING
IN
NAINITAL REGION

About the Editors

Dr. S.K. Singh passed his M.A. and Ph.D. (BHU) in Geography. He is now Reader in the Department of Geography, Kumaun University Campus, Almora. He has been a co-editor of the book on *Geography and Environment: Issues and Challenges* published from the Concept. Dr. Singh is actively engaged in geographical, environmental and development issues in Kumaun region. He has supervised several Ph.D. level researches under him on the related topics including tourism. He is author of over 40 research papers.

Dr. P. Nag passed M.Sc. and Ph.D. from BHU. He was the Chairman of the ICA Commission on Population Cartography and Member of the IGU Commission on Population Geography. At present he is the Director of the National Atlas and Thematic Mapping Organisation. He is also the President of the Indian National Cartographic Association and the Indian Association of Special Libraries and Information Centres. Dr. nag has brought out several books.

Research Team

The research team belong to the Department of Geography of Kumaun University, Almora who have been working as research scholars and associates with Dr. S.K. Singh.

TOURISM AND TREKKING IN NAINITAL REGION

Edited by

DR. S. K. SINGH
and
DR. P. NAG

Research Team

Dr. (Mrs.) Santosh Verma
Dr. Ajay Kumar Singh
Dr. M.S. Chauhan
Shri R. U. Sukala
Mrs. Savita Singh

Published in Collaboration with
PROF. S. P. CHATTERJEE MEMORIAL FOUNDATION CALCUTTA

By

CONCEPT PUBLISHING COMPANY, NEW DELHI - 110059

ISBN. 81-7022-769-0

First Published 1999

Published and Printed by
Ashok Kumar Mittal
Concept Publishing Company
A/15-16, Commercial Block, Mohan Garden
New Delhi-110059 (India)

Phones : 5648039, 5649024
Fax : 091-11-5648093

DEDICATED

to

Shri Anil Kumar Kundu

Former Director
National Atlas and Thematic
Mapping Organisation
Calcutta

PREFACE

From time immemorial travel has been fascinating and also a source of pleasure for the human being. In ancient times, the travellers were merchants, pilgrims, seekers of knowledge, adventurers and others who were desirous to seek new exciting experiences of a varieties of land and people. Thus travel is not a recent phenomenon, while tourism is relatively considered to be a modern development. Tourism can be distinguished by its mass character in the present age. A few travellers went out in the past for business and other purposes. Due to the development of science and technological advancements, travel has been diversified in the form of pleasure and recreational tourism.

Since last two decades, the study of tourism is undergoing remarkable transformation both in its contents and research, as well as its methodology and approaches. There has been almost a revolution in the field of information, ideas and concepts, intellectual awareness and related applied aspects. As a result there has been a great offshoot in the study of tourism. It is based on much more conceptual and empirical evolution. However, this particular field has come of age both in the field of theoretical constructs and approaches. Some scientific works on tourism are being carried out in various countries of the world, specially in the U.S., U.K., Germany and Japan. Such progress and achievements have also influenced India in view of economic progress, and, as such, a good number of articles as well as monographs have come out.

The relevance of tourism, as an important factor in the growth and development, has been recognised as a post-second world war phenomenon. The want for thrilling experiences is more in the affluent societies. Tourism is generally considered as a social movement with a view of having rest and relaxation, appreciation and enjoyment of natural as well as cultural attributes. From the level of scattered wandering of elite and some inquisitive and courageous people, it has now developed into a mass travel phenomenon. The factors which influence these movements are due to the growing demand for the increase in income, liberty, leisure; technical and scientific advancements and improved facilities. It involves hotel and catering industries, transportation and travel agencies, suppliers of goods and services for hoteliers, holiday resorts, entertainment and souvenir industry, etc.

The present study of tourism in Nainital region has been selected because of its unique personality and characteristics for the development of tourism, and also for its unique geographical and environmental background. This study region is partly from Nainital and partly from Almora district of the northern Indian State of Uttar Pradesh. There are eighteen development blocks in the study region, namely, Okhlakanda, Baitalghat, Ramgarh, Bhimtal, Dhari, Kotabagh, Haldwani and Ramnagar of Nainital district; and Tukula, Dhauladevi, Bhaisiyachhana, Lumgara, Hawalbagh, Gurur-Baijnath, Bageshwar, Chaukhutia, Tarikhet and Dwarahat blocks of Almora district. In this Himalayan region, Katryuris were the first Aryan who introduced settled life and agriculture, and thus a started a new dimension in the cultural scene. Its unique physiographic characteristics, and hilly topography consists of forests, river basins, valleys and water divides which have attracted persons from all walks of life.

The aim of this volume is to analyse (a) the nature of tourism, (b) to highlight the issues involved, and (c) to evolve a healthy relationship between the environmental factors and tourism. Further the study aims to bring out the potentialities of the region which may help in further improvement. To a great extent, this study is based on the fieldwork and personal survey. In order to know the pattern of tourism, the understanding of the physio-cultural features is however essential. But it is rather difficult to observe all these aspects of tourism in the relatively remoter part of the country.

The field study was limited to the places of tourist potential. Nevertheless, one has to depend on various records such as gazetteers, travelogues and the like. The socio-economic and cultural features have been compiled from folklorists, government offices, old published literature and with the assistance of elder people. Further, in order to know the demographic characteristics, district gazetteers, censuses, statistical handbooks of different years were consulted. The details of civic amenities and public utility services, which have been provided to the local people as well as for the tourists were recorded from different offices. In order to enquire about the functional and behaviour aspects of tourist, information regarding typology or tourists (domestic and international), purpose of visit, age-sex structure, mode of travel, type of accommodation, income and expenditure, field surveys were carried out in different seasons which helped in perceiving the intricacies of the phenomenon of tourism in this ancient region. On the other hand, the environmental parameters were highlighted by Dr. R.P. Singh, Head, Department of Forestry, Kumaun University, Nainital. We were also encouraged by Professor J.S. Singh, Department of Botany, Banaras Hindu University (BHU), Varanasi; Professor S.P. Singh, Department of Botany, Kumaun University, Nainital; Professor O.P. Singh, Department of Geography, Kumaun University, Nainital, Professor S.L. Kayastha, Department of Geography, BHU, Varanasi, and Dr. D.K. Mittra of National Library, Calcutta.

In a way this volume is of historical importance as well. It will be the first publication of the Professor S.P. Chatterjee Memorial Foundation which has recently been established in Calcutta in honour of the great geographer-cartographer of our times. Further, we would like to dedicate this volume to Shri A.K. Kundu, former Director of the National Atlas and Thematic Mapping Organisation (NATMO), Calcutta who was instrumental in bringing out the *Tourist Atlas of India*, we have always been encouraged by him in our endeavours.

Apart from the academic support, we were also facilitated by the administrators of the region, particularly Shri Keshav Desh Raju, IAS, and Shri D. Dipti Bilas, IAS, both District Magistrates of Almora. We are also grateful to the Directorate of Tourism, Lucknow; Hill Development Corporation, Lucknow; Kumaun Mandal Vikas Nigam Ltd., Nainital; Regional Tourist Officer, Nainital and the Tourist Bureau of Almora, Ranikhet and Ramnagar for providing relevant information and facilities to carry out the fieldwork.

We deeply express our sincere thanks to our Research Team for the fieldwork. We also thank their colleagues and friends to encourage and help them in completing this work. The Concept Publishing Company has always supported us in our initiatives. We are thankful to Shri Naurang Rai and Shri Ashok Kumar for taking great pains in completing this publication in time.

23rd July, 1997
Almora/Calcutta

S.K. SINGH
and
P. NAG

CONTENTS

Preface 7
List of Figures 12
List of Tables 14
List of Coloured Plates 15

1. Introduction 17
2. Geographical Background 26
3. Places of Tourist Interest 48
4. Socio-economic and Cultural Dimensions 88
5. Civic Amenities and Public Utility Services 102
6. Tourist Response and Preferences 118
7. Adventure Tourism: Trekking 137
8. Epilogue 158

Appendices

I. Mean monthly temperature at different resorts in the Nainital region 169
II. Mean monthly distribution of rainfall at different resorts in the Nainital region 170
III. Tourism traffic in Jim Corbett National Park. 171
IV. Instructions to the Trekkers by the Indian Mountain Federation 172
V. India at a glance 174
VI. Foriegn Tourists visiting India 176

Bibliography 177
Index 183

LIST OF FIGURES

2.1	Nainital Region: Administrative units and its Surrounding Area	27
2.2	Contours in Nainital Region	28
2.3	Physiography and Physical Divisions	31
2.4	Drainage	32
2.5	Vegetation	35
2.6A	Conditions of Atmosphere: Hythergraph (Nainital and Almora)	37
2.6B	Conditions of Atmosphere: Hythergraph (Mukteshwar and Ranikhet)	38
2.7	Temperature in different Centres	39
2.8	Classification of Tourist Centres	45
3.1	Nainital Region: Distribution of Tourist Centres	49
3.2	Guide Map of Nainital Town	50
3.3	Excursion Places around Nainital	51
3.4	Nainital: Excursion	55
3.5	Almora: Guide Map	57
3.6	Excursion Places of Almora	59
3.7	Guide Map of Jim Corbett National Park	66
3.8	Ranikhet	74
3.9	Kausani	75
3.10	Bhowali	79
3.11	Mukteshwar	86
4.1	Nainital Region: Places of Socio-cultural Interest	89
5.1	Nainital Region: Civic Amenities	103
5.2	Transport system in Nainital Region	105
6.1	Categories of Tourists According to Religion, Income and Occupation	120
6.2	Origin of Tourists: National and International	122
6.3	Aspects of Tourism: Tourists and their visiting purpose	125
6.4	Distribution of Tourists according to their Age and Sex Structure	126

6.5	Mode of Travel	129
6.6	Types of Accommodations in the Region	131
6.7	Tourist visits during Different Seasons (Based on income group)	132
7.1	Trekking Resorts in Lesser Himalayan Region	148
7.2	Route Map of Glaciers	151
8.1	Nainital Region: Proposed Planning for Tourism Development	159
8.2	Nainital Region: Tourist Complexes	163

Tyagi, N. (1982), A geographical study of Hill Resorts in U.P. Himalayas, Ph.D. thesis, Gorakhpur University, Gorakhpur (unpublished).

Wall, G. and Wright, C. (1977), *The Environmental Impact on Outdoor Recreation*, Department of Geography, Publication Series No. 11, University of Waterloo, Waterloo.

LIST OF TABLES

1.1 :	Recreational Activities in Nainital Region	24
2.1 :	Major Natural Lakes in the Region	34
2.2 :	Relationship between Rainfall and Slope	36
2.3 :	Classification of Tourist Centres	44
3.1 :	Places of Tourist Interest in and around Nainital	52
3.2 :	Places of Tourists Interest in and around Almora	58
3.3 :	Climatic Condition of the Jim Corbett National Park	63
3.4 :	Visibility of Wildlife in the Jim Corbett National Park	64
3.5 :	Accommodation in Jim Corbett National Park	65
3.6 :	Views of Snowy Himalayan Peaks from Ranikhet	69
3.7 :	Places of Tourist Interest in and around Ranikhet	71
3.8 :	Places of Tourist Interest in and around Bhimtal	78
4.1 :	Nature of Expenditure (1986)	99
4.2 :	Income of Nainital and Almora Municipal Boards from Passenger Toll Tax	100
5.1 :	Distribution of Metalled Roads (km)	106
5.2 :	Accommodation in Nainital and Almora Towns	109
5.3 :	Electric Connections in Nainital and Almora Towns	111
5.4 :	Water connection in Almora and Nainital Towns	112
5.5 :	Educational Institutions	114
6.1 :	Religion and Tourism	119
6.2 :	Occupation of Tourists	121
6.3 :	Tourism and Income Levels	121
6.4 :	Domestic and international Tourists	123
6.5 :	Tourists and Purpose of Visits	124
6.6 :	Tourists according to Age-groups	127
6.7 :	Mode of Travel of the Tourists	129
6.8 :	Type of Accommodation availed	130
6.9 :	Income Groups of the Tourists	133
7.1 :	Checklist for Trekkers	142
7.2 :	Trekking Spots around Nainital	149
8.1 :	Tentative Diffusion of Tourist Activity in the Lake Basin	164

LIST OF COLOURED PLATES (PHOTOGRAPHS)

1		Nainital – A Heaven for Tourist	33
2	A	A Distant View of Trishul and Nandakhat alongwith Lush Green Forests,Ranikhet (Almora).	40
	B	The Tranquil Naini Lake – Nainital	40
3	A	Confluence of Saru and Gomti Rivers at Bageshwar	53
	B	Kausani in Winters	53
4	A	Dense Forest at Syyahidevi (Almora)	60
	B	A Lush Green Wood-land	60
5	A	Panoramic View of Almora Township	73
	B	Ranikhet Township alongwith its Sylvan Environs	73
6	A	Bird's Eye View of Bhowali	76
	B	Picturesque Bhimtal with an Island Inside the Lake	76
7	A	Jageshwar Temple Complex, (Almora)	81
	B	'Sun Temple' Cluster of Katarmal (Almora)	81
8		A Historic Remnant of Chand Dynasty: A Gusardeval Temple, Dwarahat (Almora)	84
9		An architectural Monument – Maha Mritunjaya Temple – Jageshwar. (Almora)	93

10	A	*Jhora* (a folk) Dancing Women in Their colourful robes	96
	B	Traditional Folk *Chholia* (Almora)	96
11	A	Enchanting Himalaya from Kausani	141
	B	Human Settlement in Rural Kumaun	141
12	A	The Sylvan Countryside around Bageshwar (Almora)	144
	B	The Flats – Nainital's Favourite meeting place.	144

Chapter 1

INTRODUCTION

Tourism is growing the world over. However, in this volume, we are more concerned about a very specialized type of tourism, i.e. the Himalayan Tourism. The beaches, water resorts and wild life centuries are all over the world. Here is the case of natural beauty, wilderness, culture and religion all blend together. The sacred and mythological shrines, places of worship, rivers, lakes and pellucid mountains have always encouraged the tourists to visit the Nainital region since time immemorial. This region has undergone several dynastic vicissitudes which lead to the formation of many petty garrison, pilgrims and administrative centres. Though some of centres vanished away in the haze of time, a few centres sustained and contributed and became places of tourist significance in the region. However, in the early days, tourism existed in different form in the region. The visitors to this region were mostly pilgrims. Kailash and Mansarovar have attracted the pilgrims who pass through the Kumaun region crossing the Lipulakh pass. The first sketch map was prepared by the Europeans in 1600 A.D. which was used by such pilgrims.

Travel to Himalaya for religion, peace and meditation has been a part of the Indian culture since ancient times. The Vedas have described tourism as *atan* which in Sanskrit means to leave home for some time and to go elsewhere. *Parayatan*, *deshatan* and *tirthatan* are still being practiced for going out to gain religious solaces.

Today tourism is considered as an industry without chimney which impresses all the sectors of the economy. Hence this economic activity is known in different ways, such as tourist business, and recreational industry and the like. This industry is the composite group of inhomogeneous services and industries (Lloyd, 1964). It included transport and travel agencies, hotel and catering industry, suppliers of a varieties of goods and services, holiday resorts, insurance companies, entertainment and souvenir industry. Department of Tourism, Government of India, uses the term 'tourism related industry' which includes the following activities:

(a) Travel agencies, tour operating agencies and tourist transport agencies,
(b) Units providing facilities for cultural or wildlife experience and adventure to tourists,
(c) Surface, air and water transport facilities for tourists,
(d) Leisure, entertainment, amusement, sports and health units for tourists, and
(e) Convention/seminar, units and organizations.

Tourism consists of three basic elements, viz. man, space and time (Wahab, 1975). These elements vary according to the distance visited by the tourist, means of transportation and the length of stay in the host area. A meaningful definition does cover the study of places, and the associated infrastructure. According to the International Union of Official Travel Organization a tourist is a person travelling for a period of twenty-four hours or more in the host country other than that in which he normally works or resides (UN, 1963). This definition would be helpful for the statistical purpose at the international level. According to Department of Tourism, Government of India, a foreign tourist is a person visiting India on a foreign passport for a period not less than 24 hours and not more than six months at a time for non-employment and non-migration and with the purpose of tourism such as pleasure, business and the like. In the present study emphasis has been given to the domestic tourist who is considered as a person who leaves his usual place and work, and goes outside for the purpose of recreation, holidaying, rest, health, sports, excursion, business, pilgrimage, conference and field study.

Tourism in India

From his book, *Geographi*, it is apparent that the great Greek philosopher Ptolemy of twelfth century was acquainted with the various cities of India. During the golden Gupta period, the Indian traders used to visit places as far as Egypt, Europe and China by sea route. The famous Chinese travellers Fayahuyan, Iventsiang, Huentsang and Itsing came to India in the period of Gupta and Harsha (606-647). They studied the religious books here. Takshashila University was the centre for learning for students for several years (700 B.C. to 700 A.D.). Scholars from the west used to reside in this university situated in Peshawar. Nalanda University situated in eastern India (Bihar) was the centre for students from the oriental countries. Huentsang and Itsing studied here for years (ASI, UD). Visits of tourists in India during that period is important in the historical perspective because civilization in this part of the world was then at its peak while most of the other parts were passing through the dark age. The cities of prehistoric age were famous for progress, prosperity, talent, taste, business, religion and trade. Such cities were Ujjain, Nasik, Airan, Ropal, Ahicchatra, Hastinapur, Kaushambi, Rajghat, Rajgarih, Patliputra, Vaishali, Maivas, Tamluk, Chandrakelugarh, Shishupalgarh, Arikamendu, Vairat, Sanchi, Sarnath, and Ratnagiri (ASI, UD). Various religious places were established by Aryans who were nomadic in nature. Further, Vaishnavism and Buddhism also contributed to religious tourism in India. In fact, this country makes a unique case of such tourism, particularly in historical sense. This aspect has been ignored by the Eurocentric contributions on India.

In the eighth century, religious tourism in India developed rapidly. Shankaracharya conceived the comprehensive form of pilgrimage. Several *maths* were established for the propagation of religious thoughts. Uttarakhand had important places of religious diffusion. Badrinath in the north, Rameshwaram in the south, Puri in the east and Dwarika in the west have had the most important *maths* of Vedic (Hindu) religion. In the same period, the Islamic religion extended great help to tourism in the Asia and Africa.

In the sixteenth century intercontinental voyages gave a new dimension to the society, consequently the knowledge gathered gave a great impetus to tourism. In this respect, Indians were much more prosperous and vigilant in Mughal period. Entertainment through tourism was limited to special groups. Indians were more habitual to take pains for religion. Feudal classes were having much resources, while common people were interested only for the purpose of spiritual and self-satisfaction.

Transport has been an elixir of tourism. Water transport helped in developing relationship by which international tourism got impetus. Industrialization laid much stress on transportation, resulting radical improvement in railways. Common people got an opportunity of travelling and subsequently new tourist destination emerged. In India, railways came into existence in 1854 and remained as a useful mode of transport till today. Indian railways ranks fourth in the world and first in Asia. It helped in the development of tourism as well. In this country, bus service is also one of the main modes of travel. This mode serves in the hill areas and plays a vital role in the economic development of the region.

Railways, buses and private cars have made distant places accessible for the common people. Air travel has also facilitated tourism. In India air service started in 1903 and got popularity after the Second World War. This mode is mainly used for saving time, and for comforts. It is possible to reach those places which are far away. Up to the time of First World War, its use was confined to defence and mail services. Air travel helped in connecting distant places and extended support to the exclusive and group tours. This type of tourism is however more popular in the western countries and Japan.

Due to above mentioned reasons, the nature of tourism has changed. In spite of various modes of travel, other reasons are also responsible for the development of tourism. In modern days, television, trekking and travels are regarded as the main sources of entertainment. Though these are not always complementary to each other. Television confines a person in a room for hours together, whereas travel gives natural pleasure of out worldly phenomena.

Nature of Tourism in Nainital

Nainital region is a part of a greater cultural and administrative unit known as Kumaun. T.G. Longstall, a famous mountaineer, has rightly mentioned that "After six visits to the snow, I shall believe that Kumaun is the most beautiful country of all in the continent of Asia. Mountains and Alps, birds and animals, butterflies and flowers all combine to make a sum of delight unsurpassed elsewhere" (Chand, 1984).

In the concerned region, a steady flow of tourist starts gradually from the second or third week of April and the period between the second-half of May and first-half of June constitute the peak period of tourist arrival in Nainital. Commencement of summer cyclones with rains in the second-half of June gradually reduces the tourist population in the region. Such a trend is repeated every year. The next tourist cycle is associated with the autumn season and remain up to the first-half of November. This season does not suffer from extremities of climatic conditions.

Nainital receives tourists from all parts of the country and abroad. But the maximum percentage of tourist arrive from western Uttar Pradesh, Haryana, Bengal, Rajasthan, Delhi, Punjab, and, southern India. Previously, the tourists in Nainital were primarily business men, executive officers, princes of different states, industrialists, but such a trend has changed. The tourists also have shorter stay at Nainital. They do come from the outlying parts of the city. The purpose of this type of visit is due to local custom, wish for the change of environment and routine life, and even for fun. In the peak period of summer season, Nainital suffered from the problem of inadequate accommodation which it has to provide to the tourists. Hotel prices increased due to lack of hotel accommodation. Shorter stay is due to this perpetual problem. Consequently, Bhimtal, Almora, Ranikhet and Kausani have become an alternative place of accommodation for the tourists. Nevertheless, cheap accommodations are scattered all around Nainital. This may help to ease the accommodation problem as well as beneficial to the tourists.

In all the places of the region, the pattern of tourist flow follow the Nainital's trend, but Corbett National Park, Haldwani and Ramnagar have different tourist cycles. This national park has certainly the best cheetal deer of Asia. It always attract foreign tourists and provides a very good view of the flora and fauna. It receives visitors throughout the year except the rainy season when accessibility becomes poor. March and April are the best months to visit here. There are substantial foreign visitors and their number is increasing every year. Students are encouraged to visit this park and accommodation at concession are available for them.

Introducing the Region

Nainital region has a unique geographical location between the Lesser Himalaya in the north and Bhabhar region in the south, lying between 28^0 30' and 30^0 north ; and 78^0 43' to 80^0 9' east . This region is bounded by Khatima, Rudrapur, Kashipur (Nainital district), and Bijnor district in the south and southwest, while in the northwest there lies Chamoli district and Syalde, Shikiasen and Salt blocks of Almora district. In the northeast and east, it is surrounded by Kapkot block of Almora district and Pithoragarh district respectively.

The names of various places in the region are derived from the combination of the physical and cultural features, such as Nainital itself has derived its name from the old temple of the Goddess Naina Devi which is built on the bank of Naini lake. The name of Bageshwar and Jogeshwar are also outcome of the famous temples of Lord Shiva, Bagnath and Jagnath respectively, while the name of Haldwani and Almora derived from plenty of availability of Hakdu trees and vegetation namely Chilmora, Kilmora and the like.

The region has a total population of about 9 lakhs and almost entire population speaks Kumauni dialect. Historically, the region remained under the influence of the Kumauni rulers but later British regime formed two separate districts of Almora and Nainital. Following this, Almora district was divided into two parts and a new district of Pithoragarh was created in 1960.

The region is dotted with beautiful centres having good weather, scenic beauty and shrines, variegated floral resources which have created great attraction for vacationists, pilgrims, scientists, trekker, mountaineers and archaeologists. Transport facilities have also provided a better opportunity to exploit the remoter tourist spots of the region. The Government of Uttar Pradesh has also provided a variety of basic facilities to the tourists. Most of the tourist resorts have been established in the Nainital region which generally experience cool climatic conditions, away from the tropical diseases. At present, a few recreational facilities are provided to attract the tourists along with all possible conveniences and interests. Table 1.1 provides some indications about the recreational activities (Singh & Kaur, 1980).

In the study region, most of the tourism and recreationl activities are concentrated around the lake basin of Nainital, Bhimtal and around Almora; while others are situated far from the major tourist centres. The lake basin of the study region have excellent natural beauty to attract a large number of tourists.

TABLE 1.1 : Recreational Activities in Nainital Region

Category	Activities
Appreciation symbolic	Sight seeing, hiking, trekking, exploring, photography, and other natural environmental activities.
Extractive symbolic	Fishing, hunting etc.
Social learning	Nature study, visiting historical and archaeological sites, trail hikes, visiting religious sites etc.
Active expressive	Games, jogging, water sports, skiing, horse riding, bird watching, forest re-orientation etc.
Passive free play	Picnicking and driving for pleasure.

Source : Singh & Kaur, 1980. Modified by the authors.

Therefore, they provided multifaced attraction to the tourists. Similarly, the snow and unique Himalayan peaks and ridges always attract the tourists for viewing from Kausani, Binsar, Chaukori and Devidhura since ages.

REFERENCES

A.S.I. (u.d.), *Archaeological Remains–Monuments and Museums*, Part 1, Archaeological Survey of India, New Delhi, p. 95.

Gist, N.P. and Fava, S.P. (1964), *Urban Society*, Crawell, New York, p. 411.

Llyod. P.J. (1964), *The Development of Tourist Industry in New Zealand*, Newzealand Institute of Economic Research (INC), Wellington, p. 11.

Mathieson, Alister and Wali, Geoffrey (1982), *Tourism : Econɔmic, Physical and Social Impacts*, Longmans, New York, p. 7.

Negi, J.S.M. (1982), *Tourism and Hoteliering – A Worldwide Industry*, Gitanjali Publishing House, New Delhi, p. 21.

Singh, T.V. and Kaur, J. (1973), The Corbett National Park, *National Herhald*, New Delhi (30th December).

Singh, T.V. and Kaur, J. (eds) (1980), *Studies in Himalayan Ecology and Development Strategies*, The English Book Stores, New Delhi, p. 202.

Whahb, S. (1975), *Tourism Management*, Tourism International Press, London, p. 8.

Chapter 2

GEOGRAPHICAL BACKGROUND

Tourism in Nainital region cannot be separated from its geographical background. As indicated earlier, the geographical, historical and cultural features have played most significant role in the development of tourism. On the other hand, the above three aspects are closely interlinked with tourism which we will discuss in the next chapter. However, tourism generally gets impetus due to soothing environmental conditions, while physical and cultural conditions have accelerated the development of the tourism.

LOCATION OF THE REGION

Nainital region of Kumaun Himalaya is composed of several smaller administrative units in the northwestern part of Uttar Pradesh. It is having a unique geographic location between main Himalaya in the north and *Bhabar* region in the south and covers an area of 4,404 sq. km. This region is bounded by Khatima, Rudrapur, Kashipur (Nainital district) and Bijnor district in the south and southwest, while in the northwest there lies Chamoli district and Syalda, Bhikiasen and Salt blocks of Almora district. In the northeast and east, it is surrounded by Kapkot block of Almora district and Pithoragarh district respectively (Fig 2.1).

Nainital is the headquarters of Kumaun and is a famous educational and tourist centre. Nainital lies towards the southeastern part of the well-known geological kroll belt of the Kumaun Himalaya which is having a number of lakes. This region consists partly of Almora and Nainital districts. There are eighteen blocks in the region, namely Okhalkanda, Baitalghat, Ramgarh, Bhimtal, Dhari, Koyabagh, Haldwani and Ramnagar of Nainital district; Takula, Dhauladevi, Bhaisiyachhana, Lumgarh, Hawalbagh, Garur-Baijnath, Bageshwar, Chaukhutia, Tarikhet and Dwarahat of Almora district. Moreover, an important and well-known tourist centre of the region is the Jim Corbett National Park which covers an area of 521 sq. km. Although an area of 313 sq. km. of the park lies in Garhwal, yet its tourist importance is primarily linked with the Nainital district.

NAINILAL REGION : ADMINISTRATIVE UNIT AND ITS SURROUNDING AREA

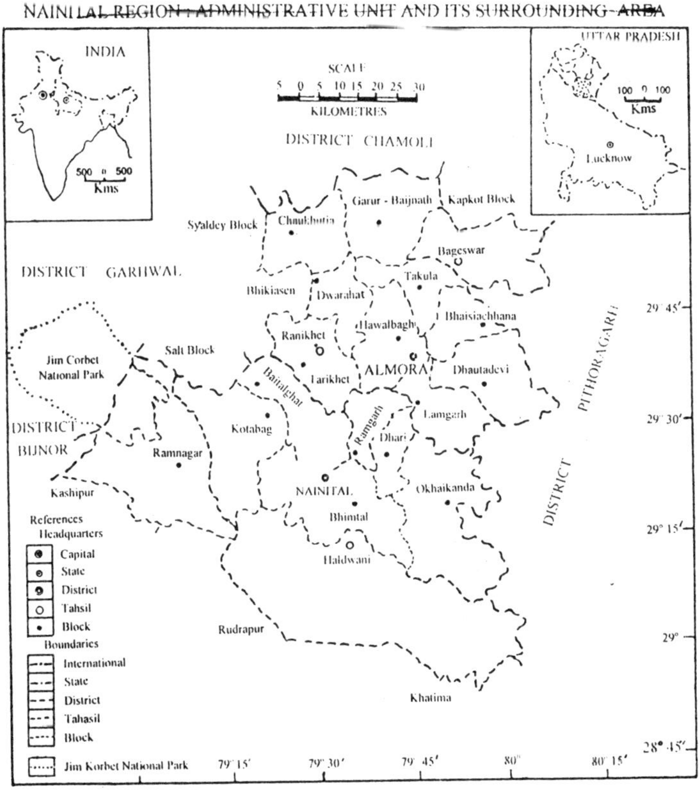

FIG. 2.1 : Nainital Region : Administrative unit and its surrounding area

PHYSIOGRAPHY

This area is considered as a region of great physical diversities, having three major physical divisions, viz. the narrow foothill belt of *Bhabar* plains in the south, Siwalik in the middle, and lesser Himalaya in the north. The altitudinal variations is the basic cause of the complexities in the landscape of the region. Considering the geology, hydrology, climate, soil, flora and fauna, it represent a distinct geographical and even cultural personality. Diversified relief, viz. numerous valleys, ridges and mountains attract many tourists to this region (Fig. 2.2).

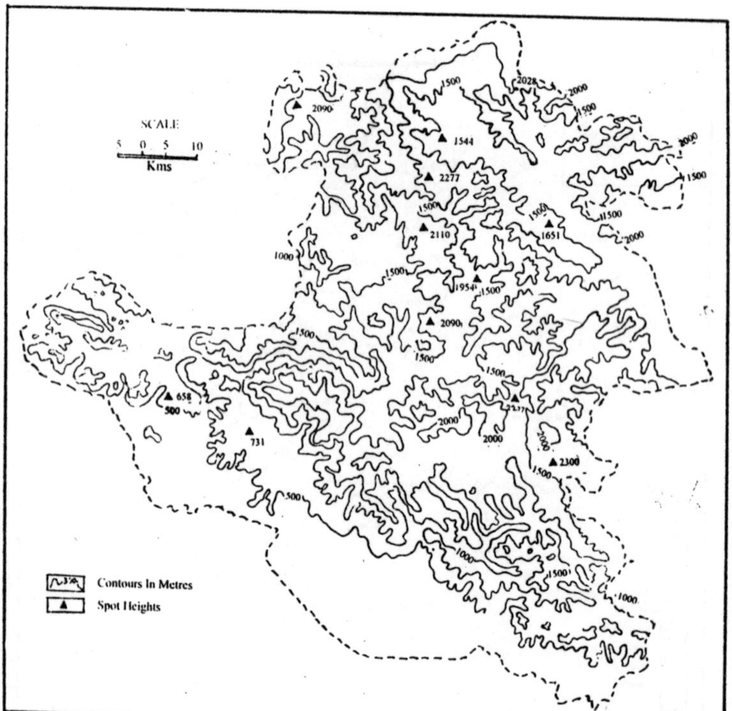

FIG. 2.2 : Contours in Nainital Region

Although several geological surveys have been conducted in different parts of the Himalayan region, but, a complete geological study could not be possible till now. Not only the geology but even the main features of the orography and geography are still not well known about the area. Some geologists like Wadia (1966), Burrard and Hayden (1907), Strachey (1951), Krishnan (1960), Pandey (1963), Gansar (1964), and Valdiya and Mishra (1961) have provided some important information about geology and geography of the region. The Siwalik belt is composed of tertiary and pleistocene deposits (Joshi, Joshi and Dani, 1983). The main rocks being sandstone, clay, conglomerates etc. while the belt of Lesser Himalaya is composed of crystalline and metamorphic rocks. Krol belt and Deoban-Tejam zone is the sub group of the latter belt. Folding, faulting and tother tectonic features can be traced in the region which are of great interest to the geologists and other earth scientists.

The geomorphic evolution of the area very clearly reveals a unique combination of factors of lithology, structure and climate. Within a small area, there exist rocks of contrast lithology each characterised by its own structural features. These rocks have reacted differently to the forces of nature and given rise to a panoramic view to the area. The geology of the region in its scientific and mineralogical sense is very interesting and attractive. There is a great future for mineral wealth in the region. For example, tungsten, a strategic mineral in Almora district, gold deposits along Jim Corbett Park, tin deposits in Jalali area of Almora district may put the region in the mineral map of India. Some other economically important minor minerals like limestone, dolomite, soapstone, magnetite and other building materials as sand, gravel and slate are of great attraction to the people for the region.

The Bhabar region is lying in the south, stretching from west to east which denotes a gravel talus with a somewhat steep slope fringing the outer margin of the hills everywhere (Wadia, 1966).

The area is densely forested, because permanent marshy and swampy conditions favour rich forestation and agricultural activities in the region. It has attractive landscape scenery, such as conjoined zones of mountains and plains, rich wild life, small springs and water channels that attract the tourists.

The region can be divided into following sub-regions based on the physiographic characteristics (Fig 2.3) :

(a) Bhabar
(b) Siwalik
(c) Lesser Himalaya

The Siwaliks are of neogene rocks and gradually rises from *Bhabar*. It is separated by the Main Boundary Fault from the Lesser Himalaya in the north (Joshi, S.C. *et al.*, 1983). Parallel ridges with thick forests are common features of this region. The Lesser Himalaya has mild and mature topography with gentle slope, providing excellent opportunity for terrace cultivation. This physiographic unit has covered a big part of the region. There is a lake basin which forms a zone about 25 km in length and 4.5 km in width (Burrard and Hayden, 1907). There are beautiful lakes offering an additional means of entertainment to the tourists. This zone also has the popular resorts of the region, such as Nainital, Almora, Ranikhet, Bhowali and Bhimtal.

DRAINAGE

The rivers of Kumaun are more active than the rivers of the other parts of the country. The diversified topography with typical lithology of the region have guided the channel flow and the structure. The region is well drained by the main rivers and their tributaries. Lakes and springs (locally known as *nalas*) are the other important features. The rivers of this region are deep, narrow and sometimes broad in accordance with lithology (Kharakwal, 1971).

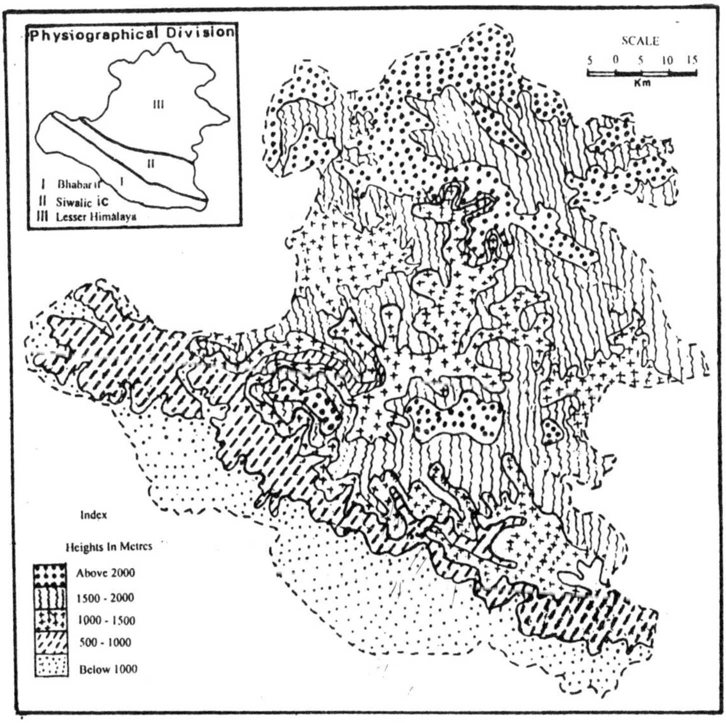

FIG. 2.3 : Physiography and Physical Diversions

The flow of water can be understood with the help of rivulets and streams. Many large and small rivulets, and perennial and seasonal streams are the characteristics of the region. Four major watershed based drainage system can be identified (Fig 2.4):

(a) Sarju-Gomti system (b) Kosi system
(c) Gola system (d) Western Ramganga-Ganga system.

Considering the tourist interest, the latter system is most important because it involves the Jim Corbett National Park. The area of this park is covered by many large and small streams, seasonal rivers and rivulets. Some of the water bodies become dry during March to June. They are Dhulwa, Kaserva, Jamnagwar, Ratapani and Pater. The main Ramganga river is the only source of water throughout the year. These water bodies and rivers have contributed to the environment of the national park for which it is so famous.

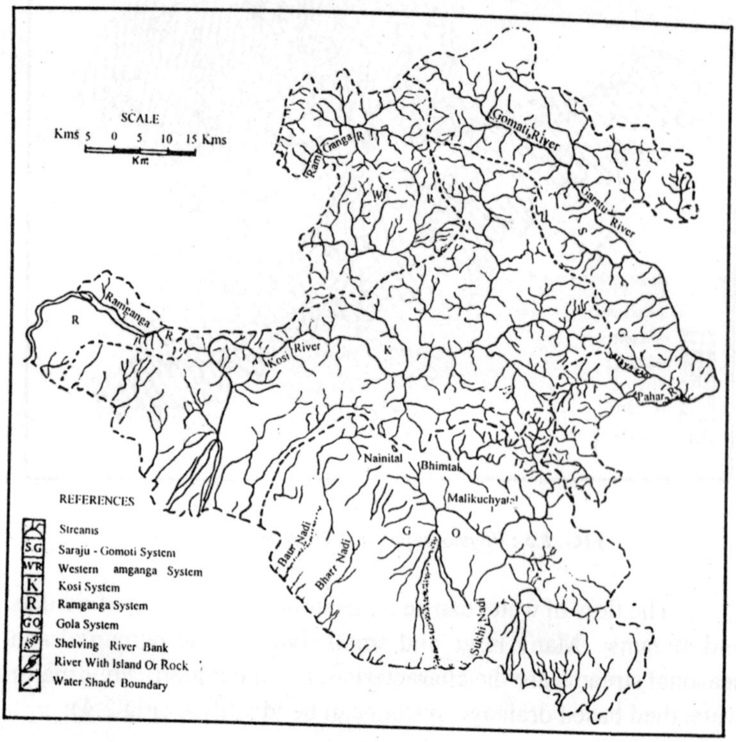

FIG. 2.4 : Drainage

LAKES

Lakes are another type of water bodies which attract tourism in the region. There are numerous lakes, but Nainital and Bhimtal are more

PLATE –I : Nainital – A haven for Tourist

significant. They have wide basins and this area is known as the Lake District of Kumaun extending about 25 km in length and 4.5 km in width. The size of these lakes is much interesting owing to paucity of such lakes in the Himalayas (Burrard *et al.*, 1907). Table 2.1 provides some basic information about the popular lakes of the region.

TABLE 2.1 : Major natural lakes in the region

Lakes	Average (m)	Maximum Length (m)	Maximum Width (m)	Maximum Depth (m)	Approx. area (sq.m)	Other information
Bhimtal	1,372	1,700.6	454.0	26.6	455,814	11.9*
Nainital	1,936	1,442.5	462.6	28.2	482,000	3492**
Nauku-chiyatal	1219	950.5	691.5	40.2	451,116.2	—
Malwatal	1,036	1,365.5	558.5	38.3	492,907	28*
Sat Tal	1,347	N.A.	N.A.	N.A.	N.A.	3.3*

* Catchment area in sq. km. ** Circumference in m.

VEGETATION

The region is very rich in flora. Lithology, chemical composition of rocks, soil, geology and altitudinal variation (<500 to >2,000 m) govern the changing mode of natural vegetation; while, the vertical distribution is controlled by isotangent surface and thermal perspective. The maximum area lies within 1,000 to 2,000 m. The vegetation in the region can be classified according to the ecosystem, which is as follows (Fig. 2.5) :

(a) Sub-tropical species (500-1,000 m)
(b) Himalayan sub-temperate forest species (1,000-1,800 m)
(c) Moist temperate deciduous species (1,800 m and above)

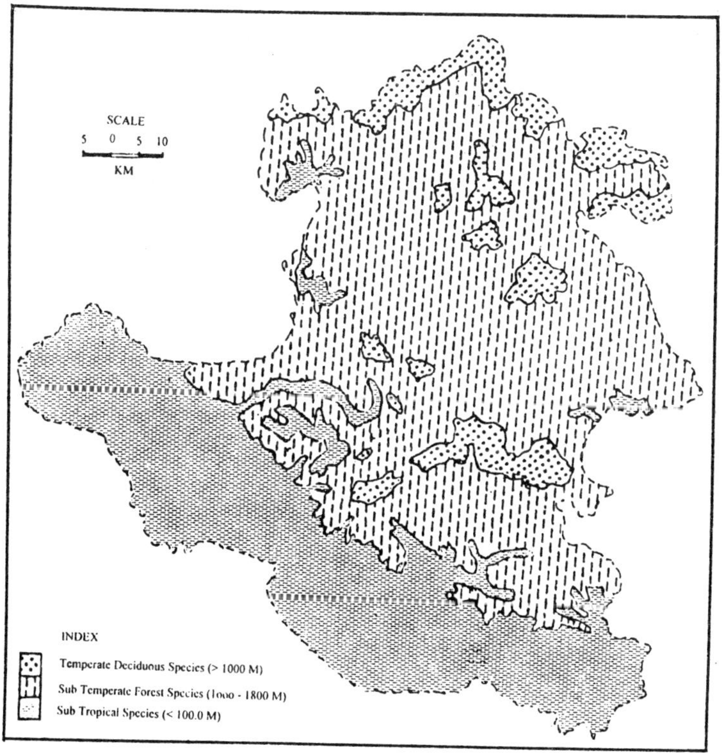

FIG. 2.5 : Vegetation

Sub-tropical deciduous forests are extending all along the southern part of the region and over the outer zone of the Siwalik range. The main species are *sal, shisham, haldu, teak, khair, eucalyptus* and *bamboo*. *Sal* is associated with *chir* in comparatively cold climate. The Himalayan subtropical forests occur in extensive patches. A wide part of the region exists under this elevation range having comparatively cool climate, deep soil and a good water conditions favourable to Pine forest. Lower variety of Oak is found almost all over the region. *Chir* forest occur in plenty in Bainjaver, Burons and Kaphal regions.

Association of pine and scrub are found along the water sources. Pine is replaced by oak in cooler climate which is favourable to banj-oak forests. Deodar is other important tree and found abundantly. The sparse distribution of *banj* and *moru* is also found in the region.

CLIMATE

The climate of the region is the composite of the weather conditions of a place throughout the year and controlled by geographical conditions, viz. location, elevation, topography and water bodies. Mountains, by virtue of their elevations, affect alignment of region, windward and leeward locations, proximity of the snow cover, water bodies or vast stretches of natural vegetation contributing to the wide differences in climatic conditions, specially regarding temperature and precipitation (Joshi, *et al.*, 1983).

Precipitation amount generally depends upon the situation of windward and leeward side of a place with respect to rain bearing winds. Therefore, the climatic conditions of one side is different from that of the other.

TABLE 2.2 : Relationship between Rainfall and slope

Centre	Altitude (m)	Rainfall (cm)	Side of the centre
Nainital	1,935	248.8	Windward
Almora	1,646	106.1	Leeward
Mukteshwar	2,275	136.0	Windward
Ranikhet	1,829	131.3	Leeward

In the concerned region, the mountainous part records low temperature for almost nine months of the year (Table 2.2). The mean monthly temperature during the month of January at Nainital, Almora, Mukteshwar and Ranikhet are 6,° 7.8°, 5.8° and 7.7°C respectively ; while at Haldwani and Ramnagar it varies between 13.2° C and 20.7°C. The temperature at lower altitudes begins to move upwards from the month of March. June is the scorching

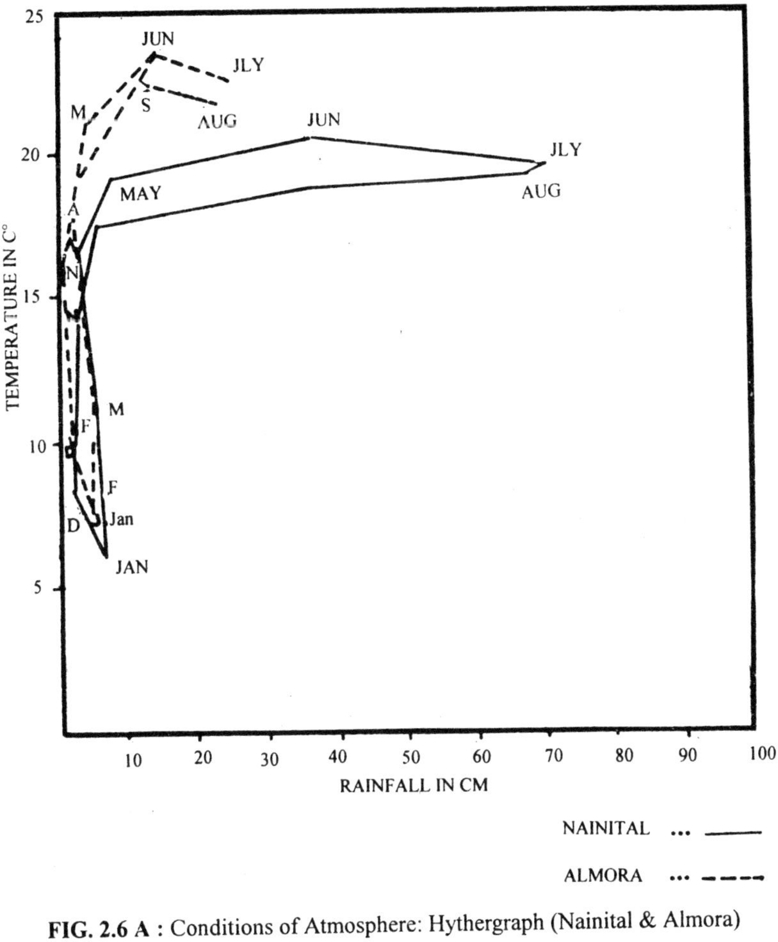

FIG. 2.6 A : Conditions of Atmosphere: Hythergraph (Nainital & Almora)

month, while high altitudes remain cool during the same month. Summer season is almost ideal for tourists in Nainital. Therefore, it was developed as a seat of administration during the British period. December, January and February offer a little discomfort due to cold, but tourists enjoy the winter months as well. In the hill resorts, there is no scorching and muggy period (Fig. 2.6A and 2.6B).

The quantity of rainfall also depends on the windward and leeward side with respect to rain bearing winds. Fig. 2.6A reveals high temperatures (23.9° C) at Almora in the month of June while Mukteshwar is coldest place having the minimum temperature of 5.8° C in the month of January. Nainital gets minimum rainfall in November (0.3 cm) while it is maximum in the month of July (70.4 cm) [Fig. 2.7].

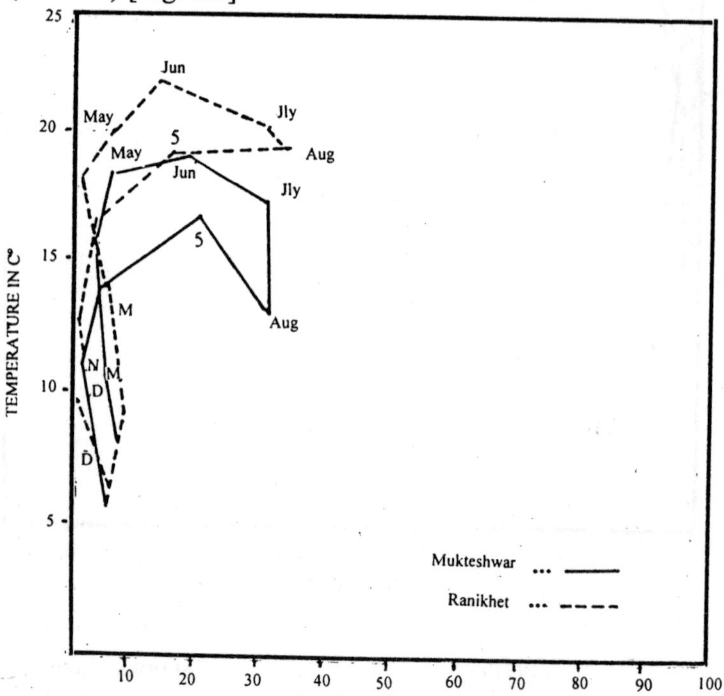

FIG. 2.6 B : Conditions of Atmosphere : Hythergraph (Mukteshwar and Ranikhet)

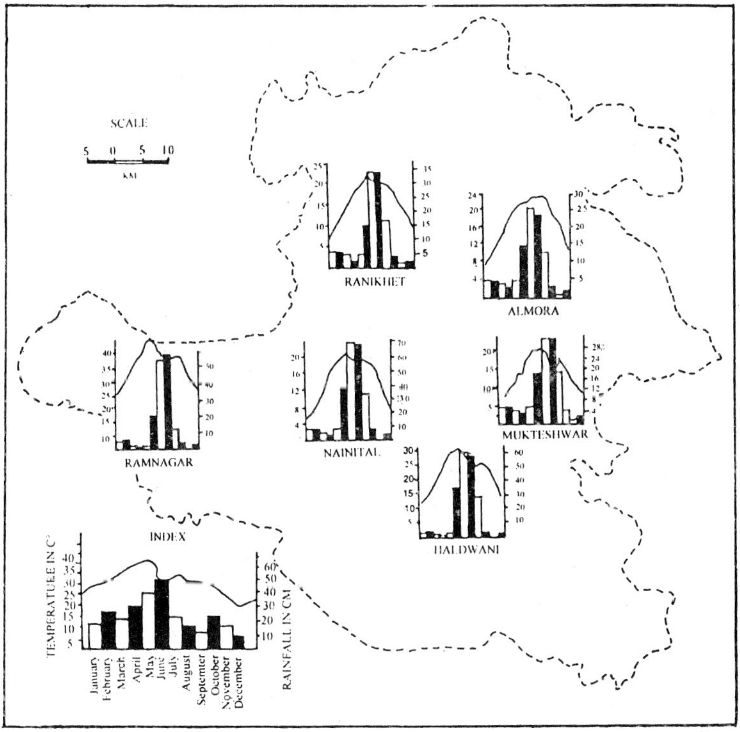

FIG. 2.7 : Temperature in different centres

Keeping in view the tourist significance, the year can be divided into the following seasons:

Cold weather season (winter)

From mid December to mid February, the weather is severely cold and monsoon conditions almost disappear. Heat of the sun during the day time and heavy dew at the night are the most significant features. There is gradual decrease in temperature which results in much cooler nights with comparatively less warmer days. January

A. Distant view of Trishul and Nandakhat alongwith lush green forests (Almora)

B. The Tranquil Naini Lake – Nainital

PLATE – II

is the coldest month with lowest temperature. Western wind disturbances bring rain in this month and February. Further, at the elevation of more than 1,500 m, the rain water tends to become solid and comes down in the form snow. This rain is important for *rabi* crops throughout the region. The foothills get rains by the drained air, therefore *Bhabar* becomes more humid than hilly region. For the same reason, frost occurs in these parts as well.

Hot weather season (summer)

In the months of March and April the temperature rises up during day time while the nights are still cold in the lower elevations. The temperature rapidly increases in these months. Further, in the months of April and May, thunderstorms and hailstorms are common. The climatic conditions are however tolerable. The nights are smooth and cold, but in the day time it becomes warm. Hot dust comes from the plains and cover the sky, therefore, the visibility becomes comparatively poor. Generally, clear sky with low humidity and occasional showers are special conditions of this season. With an exception of a few local showers, the weather is almost dry; and due to this, dry heat becomes very conspicuous. The hot summer wind known locally as *Loo* is experienced in *Bhabar* region.

Rainy season (southwest monsoon)

After the second week of June, the region usually comes under the grip of monsoon. Hot and dry weather changes into a season of high atmospheric activities and result into heavy rains. The temperatures also falls quite considerably till September. The distribution of rainfall during these months depends upon the shift of axis of the trough of low air pressure over northern India. When this axis shifts towards south, it causes heavy rains over the hills. However, while moving northwards, the condition is diverse. The rainy months are July and August. Almost 80 per cent of annual precipitation obtained during these months is from the southwest monsoon which have usually minimum velocity. Nevertheless, several local factors disturb this system.

Retreating monsoon season (autumn)

By the month of September, the rainfall, after long intervals, scatters because of the comparatively weakened monsoon. The weather becomes clear and winter starts with bright atmosphere, clear sky, sharp nights and thick dew. This condition prevails till the beginning of February. With retreat of monsoon, the winds assume north-east, north and northwestern turn. The sky is now clear and with low humidity. There is a general decline in temperature specially during the later month which ultimately results into the onset of the winter season.

ORIGIN OF TOURIST CENTRES

The Nainital region of the state of Uttar Pradesh has much possibilities for the development of tourism. Its diversified landscape with its patrimonial culture and cultural life, tradition, folk art, fairs and festivals always attract people from various places. The rock shelter paintings with the layer of brunt of clay in various mountainous ranges and bottoms of some valleys of lower slopes, ruined rock edicts are still witnesses of nature of human activities of the early historic period. During the Aryan period, other outsiders also inhabited this region, viz. Kiratas, Rajya Kiratas, Sakas, Khasas, Nagas and Hyunas. After Harsha, there was a period of local chiefs (Nautyal, 1969).

Since the early historic period, various dynasties had ruled over this region. The Katyuris has a long dynastic history. Generally the folk culture of present Kumauni traditions are the gift of this period. This dynasty had migrated from Katyur valley known as *Kartikeyapura* (Baijnath-Garur) valley of Almora district (Nautyal,

1969). The sacred Jageshwar was selected for religious construction by the famous Katyuri king named Basantan Deva. Bageshwar and Baijnath shrines of this region were also established by this dynasty. This period is still well remembered for construction activities as well as for the development of roads and agricultural settlements. Their style of art and architecture can be noticed in the temple clusters of Jageshwar, Bageshwar, Baijnath and Dwarahat (Pande, 1990).

The Chands came to rule over this region after Katyuris had established themselves near Champawat, now in Pithoragarh district (Nautyal, 1969). Almora was established in 1563 A.D. later, it became an important administrative and cultural centre. Some of the towns of *tarai* originated even later. The last successful ruler of this dynasty was Raja Udyot Chand, after whom the Chanda gradually lost their monarchy.

With the changing fortunes of the Chand dynasty, the region came under Gorkha who conquered Almora in 1790 A.D. (Pande, 1990). They wended almost all parts of Kumaun, and *Bhabar tarai* region. It is said that they ruled with a "rod of iron". They first introduced the settlement of the land revenue and also imposed taxes on cultivated land and even on the population to meet the expenses of their establishments (Etkinson, 1974). The tendency of territorial expansion of the Gorkhas lead to their conflict with the British, as a result they lost their dominance in 1815 A.D.

After then agreement of Sigauli with the Gorkhas in the same year (1815 A.D.), the Britishers expanded the activities of the East India Company, and established their commercial centres near *Terai Bhabar* (Pande, 1990). In 1839, the Kumaun region, comprising of Almora and Nainital districts, was separated from Garhwal and gradually came under their administrative control (Vashnava, 1983). The *Bhabar-Terai* tract was of full of tiger, elephant and other dreadful animals. During British period, this region was transformed due to political reasons suitable to the colonial rulers.

TABLE 2.3 : Classification of tourist centres

Type	Tourist Centres
1. Hill resort	Nainital, Almora, Kausani, Bhowali, Ranikhet and Bhimtal.
2. Lake resorts	Nainital and Bhimtal
3. Gateway town (Transport points)	Haldwani, Kathgodam and Ramnagar.
4. Religious centres	Jageshwar, Bageshwar, Jaijmath and Dwarahat.
5. Centre of excellence in architecture.	Baijnath, Bageshwar, Katarmal, Almora and Dwarahat.
6. Sanctuary centre	Ramnagar
7. Town with beautiful orchards	Ramnagar, Bhowali, Mukteshwar, Chaubatia, Ranikhet and Jalan.
8. Military towns	Ranikhet Nainital and Almora Cantonment.
9. Centre of education	Nainital, Ghorakhal, Almora, Ranikhet, Bageshwar and Dwarahat.

Development of transportation, communication, education, health and commerce reveals such intentions. A new era in urban history of U.P. Himalaya began after India got independence in 1947. In the following year, the state of *Terai* was incorporated with Kumaun commissionary as a separate district. In 1960 new administrative boundaries were made after the reorganization of the district. A separate division, known as Uttarakhand, was created out of the existing district (Tehri, Garhwal and Almora). All the parts, comprising three districts of Uttar Kashi, Chamoli and Pithoragarh, bordering Tibet, were put under this division. Several new towns came in existence after reorganization. The Government took keen interest in the development of this area through various schemes. Companies, industries and power generation, agriculture and other aspects of development came in existence as a part of the national Five Year plans. After partition of the country (1947), the state government had rehabilitated the refugees from Pakistan and later from Bangladesh (1972) in *Terai Bhabar* region along the foothills. In addition, army pensioners, landless labourers and freedom fighters have also been settled here from 1947 onwards. Various towns have also been settled, for example Haldwani-Kathgodam and Ramnagar showed rapid development due to rich agricultural

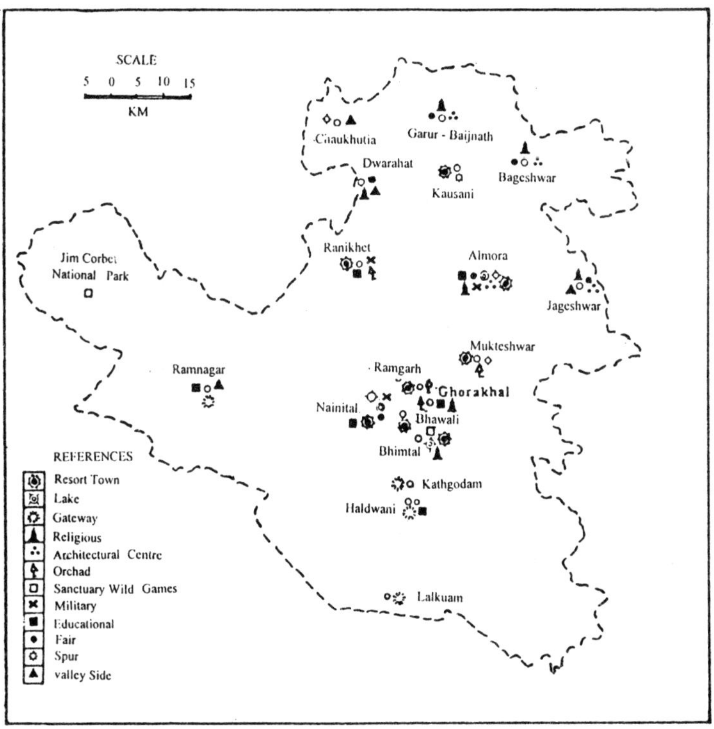

FIG. 2.8 : Classification of Tourist Centres

environment, facilities of transport and communication. The year 1970 is the period of multiple progress (Table 2.3). Almora, Nainital Haldwani-Kathgodam have crossed their carrying capacity, but the mountainous region lags behind. The towns of lesser Himalayan region developed faster due to tourism (Tiwari & Singh, 1983). Some other small centres are also developing however at a slower pace. In general, the centres of tourist interest which came into existence with their natural beauty, site and other attractions may broadly be classified as follows (Fig. 2.8).

Keeping in view the foregoing characters of the hill resorts in the region, it may be noted that most of the resorts are newly developed. Now the region has been able to enhance its distinctive tourist image. Even a few resorts have appeared on the world map of tourism due to their unique personality. From the geographical point of view they provide interesting combination of location and morphology.

REFERENCES

Burrard, S.G. and Hayden, H.H. (1907), *A sketch of the Geography and Geology of Himalayan Mountains and Tibet*, Pt. 3, Government of India Press, Calcutta.

Etkinson, E.T. (1974), *Kumaun Hills*, Cosmo Publication, Delhi.

Joshi, S.C., Joshi, D.R. and Dani, D.D. (1983), *Kumaun Himalaya: A Geographic Perspective on Resource Development*, Gyanodaya Prakashan, Nainital.

Kharakwal, S.C. (1971), The U.P. Himalaya, in R.L. Singh *et el.* (eds), *India – A Regional Geography*, National Geographical Society of India Publication, Varanasi.

Nag, P. and Sengupta, S. (1992), *Geography of India*, Concept Publishing Company, New Delhi.

Nautiyal, K.P. (1969), *The Archaeology of Kumaun*, Chaukhamba Sanskrit Series, Varanasi.

Pande, B.D. (1990), *Kumaun ka Itihas*, Shree Almora Book Depot, Almora.

Tewari, M.M. and Singh, S.K. (1983), The urban fact of U.P. Himalaya in Historical Perspective, in O.P. Singh (ed), *The U.P. Himalaya: Nature, Man and Culture*, Rajesh Publication, New Delhi.

Vashnava, Y.D. (1983), *Himalayan Districts–Land and People of Uttar Pradesh*, Almora Book Depot, Almora.

Wadia, D.N. (1966), *Geology of India*, ELBS MaçMillian & Co.Ltd., London.

Chapter 3

PLACES OF TOURIST INTEREST

With beautiful natural conditions and availability of all sorts of modern comforts, the hill resorts of the Nainital region are much popular among the domestic and international tourists. Unique characteristics of climate and physical features constitute the backbone of tourist industry of this region. Temperate climate during summer attracts a large number of tourists towards this region which is also rich in archaeological, historical, artistic and cultural attributes. Round the year, the glory of Nainital, Ranikhet, Kausani and Almora are well-known. Then there are places like Jageshwar and Bageshwar which have close association with holy sites like Baijnath. Bhimtal is also famous for cluster of natural lakes while Kausani and Ranikhet provide unique pleasure of viewing Himalaya. Mukteshwar-Ramgarh tracks do offer fruitful recreation to tourists and in fact Nainital offer a wide choice of activities which suits practically all tastes and age groups (Fig. 3.1). The description of the important places will provide necessary details for tourism.

Nainital

Nainital (29^0 23' N and 79^0 33' E) is one of the most picturesque, well maintained, and attractive tourist resort of the Himalayan region. It was the summer seat of administration of the Government of United Provinces. The secretariat of this government used to shift here for three months from Lucknow every year up to 1947, and later from 1947 to 1962 it was for two months only. However, Uttar Pradesh government has stopped this hill exodus in the following years. At present, only the governor comes here for two months during the summer, and often for a few weeks during the autumn. Short trips to Lucknow are made from time to time. Many government offices have now been established in the Old Secretariat building.

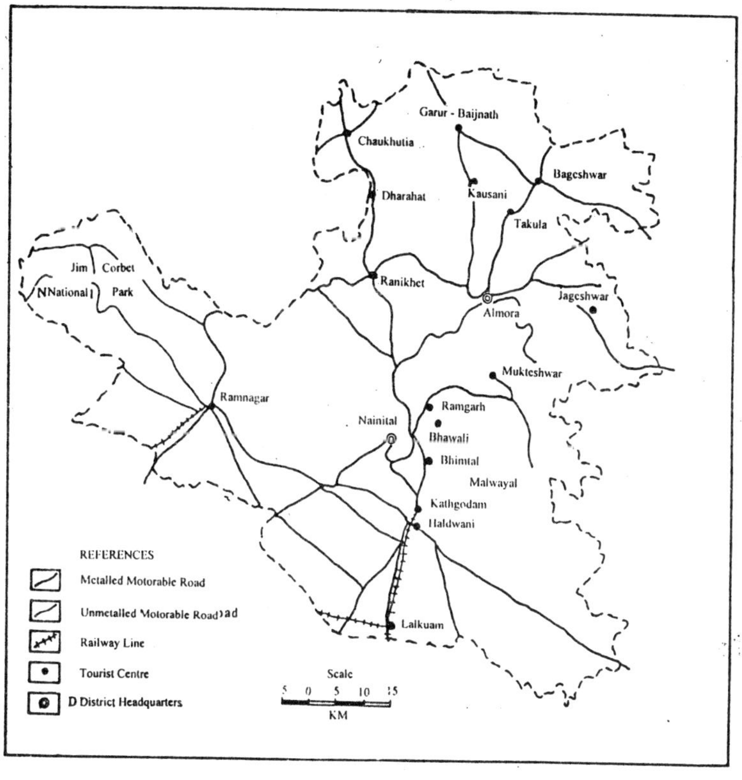

FIG. 3.1 : Nainital Region : Distribution of Tourist Centres

Its name has been derived from the Naini Lake and Goddess Naina Devi. The *Tal* is synonymous with lake. This place is mentioned in Manaskhanda of the *Skanda Puran* as *Tririshi Sarovara* or the lake of three *Rishis* (saints) : Atri, Pulastya and Pulaha (Atkinson, 1982-84). Mr. P. Barron discovered this place in 1839, when he came here for hunting from Kaladhungi. He appreciated the charming, attractive and beautiful natural lake at this place. After its discovery, this place has undergone rapid progress and now it has become one of the most popular hill resorts of India with cosmopolitan hospitality and amenities. In 1960 the Government of Uttar Pradesh opened a tourist bureau in Nainital to promote tourist related activities in the town and area around it. This town covers an area of 11.75 sq. km. including the lake. It is 1,935 metres above the sea level. The population of the town in 1991was about 30 thousand.

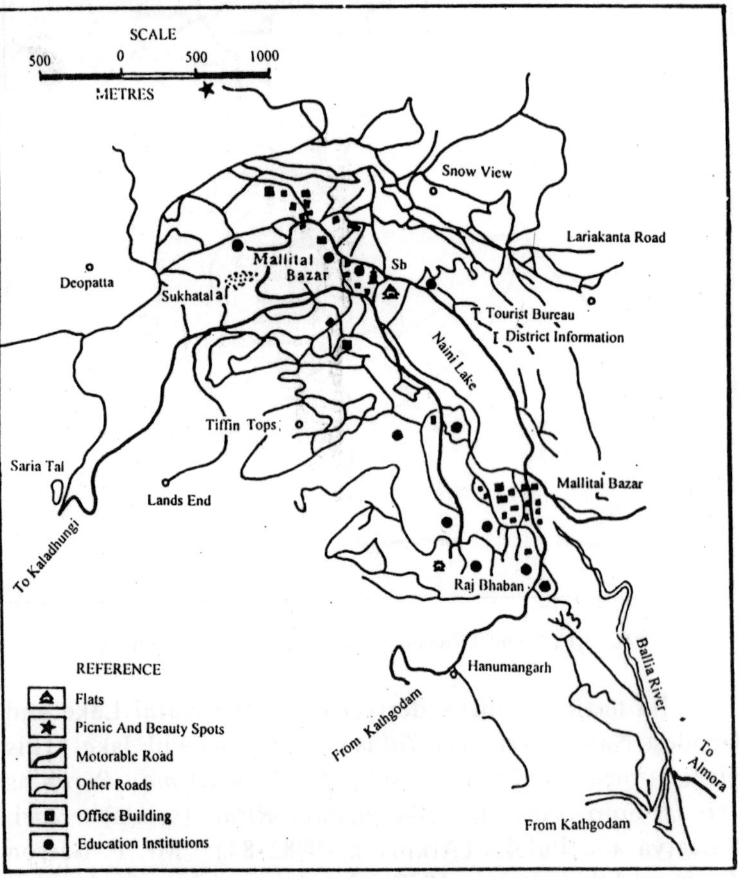

FIG. 3.2 : Guide Map of Nainital Town

The Britishers gave all possible touch of the western style to this town. The Kumaun culture of east with the influence of the western culture has given a unique personality to this resort town. But visitors, flower beds, gardens, hotels, bungalows, public schools and colleges and western architecture are common sight here.

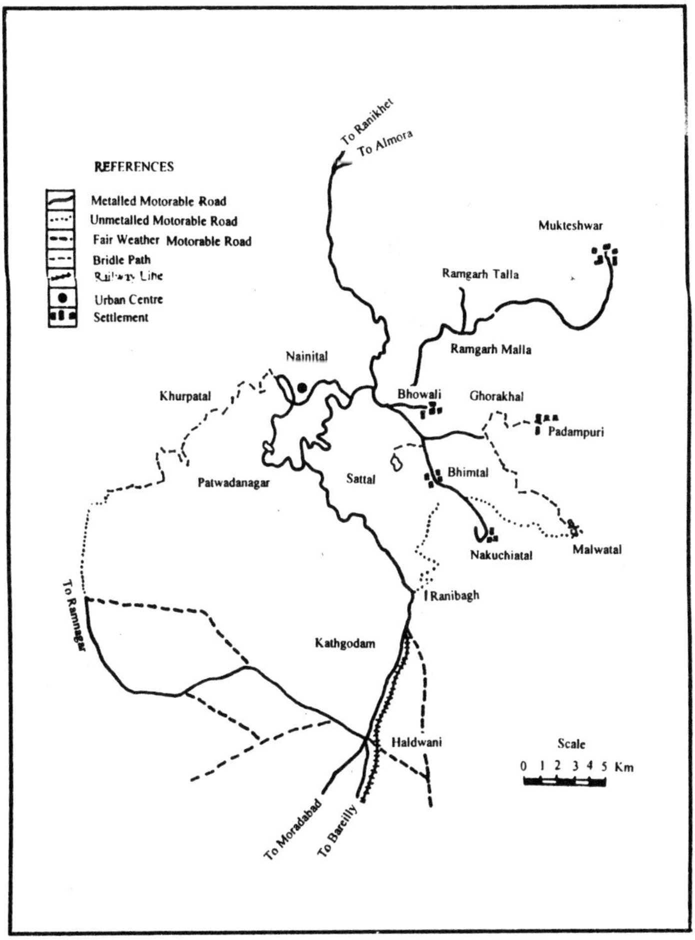

FIG. 3.3 : Excursion Places Around Nainital

Stretching from south to north of the lake, the town has two main markets connected with The Mall. The Mallital market is spread over the northwest end of the lake while the southeast end is surrounded by Tallital market. Forests full of oak trees have covered the top. Mainly Mallital is dominated by hotels, cafes, restaurants and other stalls. A number of colleges, dormitories, villas, guest houses and clubs are also situated in different parts of the town (Fig. 3.2).

The natural beauty of Nainital is exceptional. The beautiful azure moss colour lake glimmering under the sun during day time while in the night it turns into a bewitching sight of attraction. The mysterious fantasy is the reflection of colourful lights dancing over the lake water. Moonlight scene in the water is also much enchanting. There are good arrangements for boating in the lake. Further, there is a wide field, spread over Mallital, known as flats. Such field, uncommon in the region, provides facilities for games and social life to the town.

The town is well-connected by road with Kathgodam (nearest rail head : 35.4 km.), Ranikhet (59 km.), Almora (68 km.), and Delhi (322 km. via Moradabad, Rampur and Haldwani). Figure 3.3 shows the places of tourists interest around this town, while Figure 3.4 within the town. Table 3.1 provides some details of such places of tourist interest.

TABLE 3.1 : Places of tourist interest in and around Nainital

Place	Altitude (m)	Distance (km.)	Special Feature	Approach
Naina Peak (China Peak)	2611	5.64	Beautiful view of Himalayas and enchanting scene of lake	Bridle path
Snow View	2270	2.42	Nice panorama of Himalaya	Bridle path

Contd.

A. Confluence of Saru and Gomti rivers at Bageshwar

B. Kausani in Winters

PLATE – III

Table 3.1 (*Contd.*)

Place	Altitude (m)	Distance (km.)	Special Feature	Approach
			is visible by telescope propounding at the peak	& ropeway
Lariakantha	2481	5.64	Attractive view of sub-urban lake region	As above
Land's End	2118	4.08	Nice view of Khurpa-tal terraced fields on the hillside	As above
Darothy seat (Tiffen Top)	2292	4.03	A memorial of an Eng--lish lady believed to have been killed in an air crash. The spot commands a sectional view of the town and nearby region.	As above
Hanuman-garhi	1951	3.22	A religious centre with an ecstatic spot well known for its sun set view.	Jeep
State Obs-ervatory	1951	4.40	Astronomical observatory and optical tracking of arti-ficial earth satellites.	Motor
Kilbury	2194	10.0	A wooded picnic spot for a quiet and peaceful holiday.	Bridle path
Khurpa Tal	1635	10.0	A fishing paradise.	As above
Bhowali	1706	11.27	Fruit market and T.B. san-atorium.	Reguler bus service
Bhimtal	1371	22.53	A captivating and delightful lake resort offering boating and picnic spot in the central island.	As above

Source : Field survey by the authors.

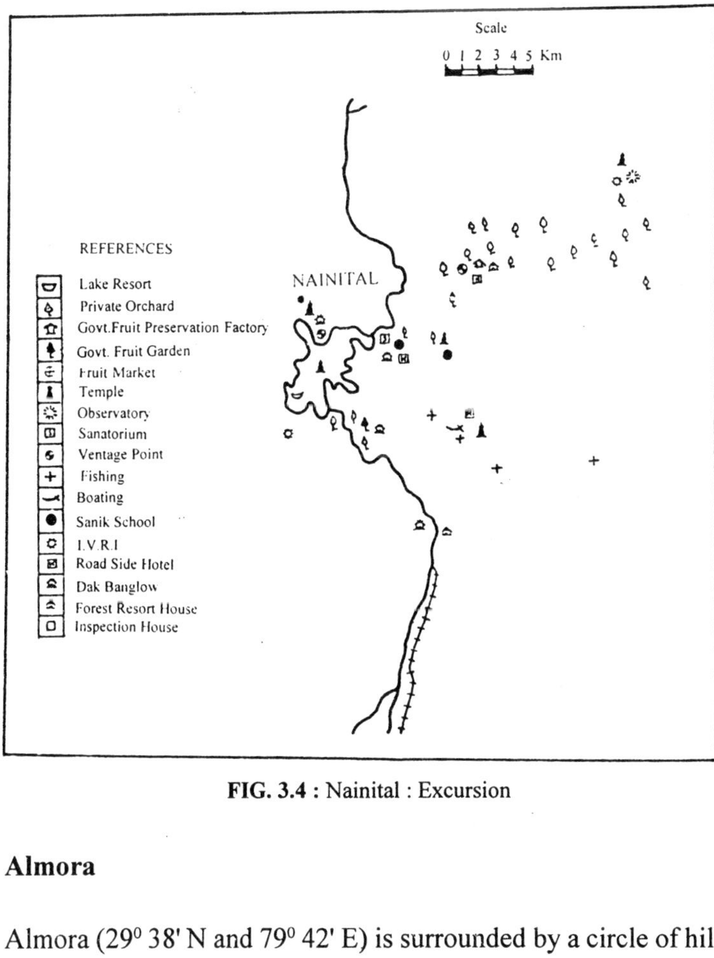

FIG. 3.4 : Nainital : Excursion

Almora

Almora (29⁰ 38' N and 79⁰ 42' E) is surrounded by a circle of hills almost each with a temple. It is an old historic town founded in 1563 A.D. by Raja Kalyan Chand of the Chand dynasty of Kumaun. It is said that once this Raja came here for hunting and a hare who presented as a tiger was followed by the king, but suddenly the tiger disappeared. With this surprise the king thought to shift his capital from Champawat (now in Pithoragarh district) to this place. From then the town became the capital of Kumaun during the Chand dynasty by the Gorkha rulers and it was headquarters of the

Commissioner of Kumaun during early British period but they reduced its status afterwards.

Spread on a long ridge it looks like a horse saddle at an altitude of 1,646 m. surrounded by various urbanized villages, particularly Khatyari, Dugalkhola, Pandekhole, Hiradungri, Baldhoti etc. These villages have already been included within the municipal board of the town. The town is generally known as trekker's resort. It covers an area of 11.9 sq km. with a population of 27,000.

This old town stands as a symbol of Kumaun's heritage. A linear market street of cobbled slate-stone runs from one end to another of the town, and straight rows of two to four runs from one end to another of the town, and straight rows of two to four storeyed houses are on either side of the road. The houses are built by stone and wood. Long slate-stone roofed houses with typical wood carvings on the doors and windows show a direct influence of nature loving artists of the area. From Almora-Ranikhet road the electric lights provides a glorious scene.

Generally tourists with intellectual bent of mind like to visit Almora. Unlike Nainital, this hill resort has received a poor tourist traffic due to lack of publicity and other tourist amenities, particularly comfortable transportation, catering, lodging, water, sanitation and recreational facilities. At present Almora's development is progressing. Tourist department is developing amenities in various parts of the town. New hotels are being constructed, roads connections are meant to ease traffic, and a new market, known as Palika Bazar, and other commercial complexes are now functioning. A holiday home has been constructed for the tourist by the state government and rest house of various departments are also providing facilities to some restricted tourists. Other hotels are trying to have more accommodation (Fig. 3.5).

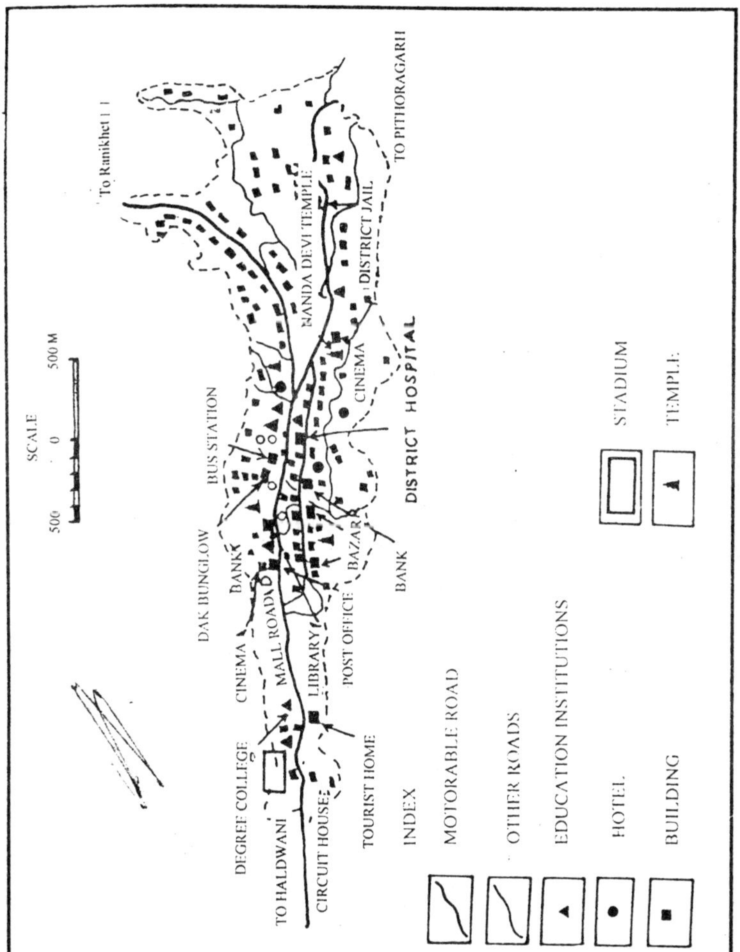

FIG. 3.5 : Almora Cuide Map

There are many temples in the town. The temple of Nandadevi is famous for the fair during autumn. The Christian mission is functioning here which has established some educational institutions. Ramakrishna Mission is located here as well. An American, Dr. Bons, came and studied the Indian religious books and built an *Ashram* on the hill of Kasardevi. Many other bungalows are situated in the town. Foreigners have been visiting this town in sufficient numbers. A famous classical and contemporary dancer of world repute, Late Sh. Uday Shankar, established here a cultural centre.

There are many religious and architectural centres existing in this district, viz. Bageshwar, Jageshwar and Baijnath, which are of more religious significance in comparison to resort for pleasure.

Almora is well connected with regular bus service from Kathgodam, Haldwani, Nainital, Ranikhet, Srinagar-Garhwal, Pithoragarh, Delhi, Ramnagar, Lucknow and Bageshwar. The nearest rail head is Kathgodam (Fig. 3.6). Table 3.2 provides information on the places of tourist interest in and around Almora.

TABLE 3.2 : Places of Tourists Interest in and around Almora

Place	Distance (km)	Special Features	Approach
Bright End Corner	1.6	View of lofty snowy peaks of Himalaya and famous for sunset.	Motor road
Matela Garden	10.4	Fruit garden	As above
Chital	12.0	Some of the Himalayan peaks are visible and famous temple of Lord Gollu	As above

Contd

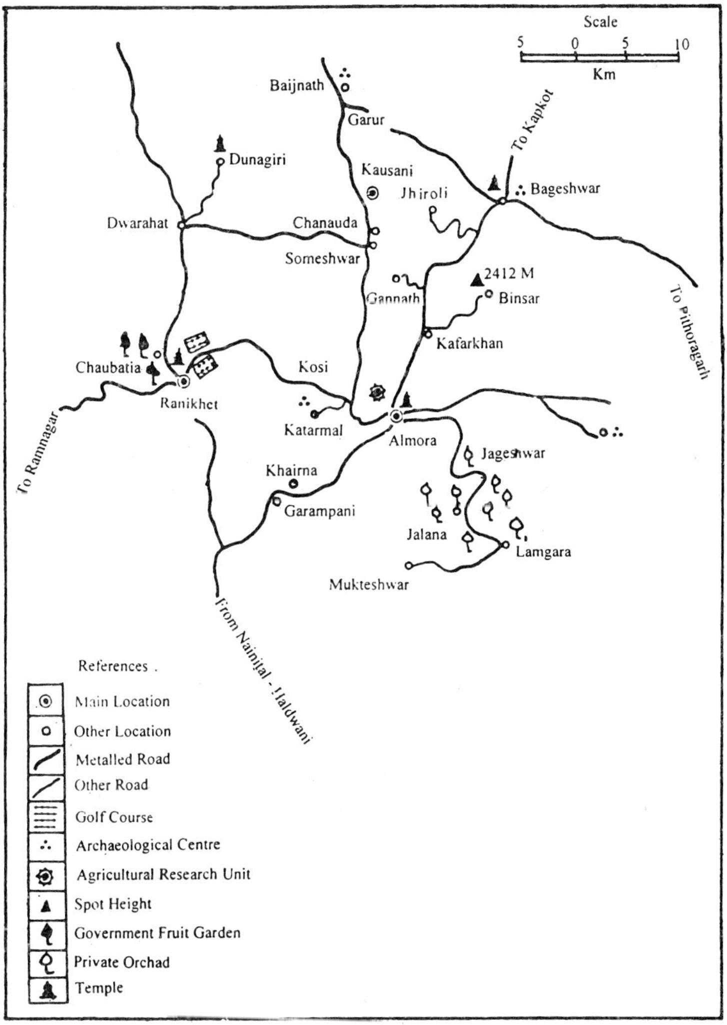

FIG. 3.6 : Excursion Places of Almora

A. Dense forest at Syyahidevi (Almora)

B. A Lush Green Wood-land

PLATE - IV

TABLE 3.2 (*Contd.*)

Place	Distance (km)	Special Features	Approach
Simtola	5.6	Natural view of hills and thick forest of pine provides beautiful landscape. It is highest peak of the town	Bridle path
Kalmattia	5.2	Famous Kasardevi temple and wonderful view of Himalaya and fruit garden etc.	Motor road
Hawalbagh	13.0	Agricultural Research Unit of ICAR.	As above
Deolly Danda	3.0	Magnificent views & temple on top of the hill.	Motor road & Bridle path
Sitoli	4.0	Agricultural research unit and temple of goddess on top of the hill	Motor road
Katarmal	17.0	Age old temple of Lord Surya and Bikut forest where forms magnificent view of Almora can be obtained	Motor road & Bridle path
Binsar	30.0	2,412 m above the M.S.L. spot for hiking, scenic beauty, Peaks of Tibetan region visible.	Jeep & bridle path
Sitalakhet	35.0	Fine views, temple of goddess and picnic spot, small hunting and camping spot of scouts	Motor road
Kausani	51.0	Famous tourist point with natural grandeur of the place	Bus service

(Contd.)

Table 3.2 (*Contd.*)

Place	Distance (km)	Special Features	Approach
Jageshwar	35.0	Age old temple clustering of Lord Shiva. Situated in a beautiful narrow valley surrounded by Deodar monarchs.	As above
Baijnath	71.0	Age old temple shrine on the bank of a river	As above
Gananath	31.0	Natural landscape, caves and Shiva temple with the fine visibility of Himalaya	Motor road
Morenaulla	91.0	Enchanting natural views and thick forests	As above
Lamgarah	35.0	Well known orchards and natural viewing of the Himalaya	As above

Source: Field survey by the authors.

Jim Corbett National Park

The Jim Corbett National Park, established in 1935, was first of its kind in India. It is located in the foothills of the outer Himalayan valley of Patalidum. It was originally named as Hailey National Park after the then governor of United Provinces, Sir Malcolm Hailey. In 1948 it was renamed as Ramganga National Park as the River Ramganga flows across the park. Finally, on first April 1973 it was rechristened as Jim Corbett National Park in order to commemorate the memory of the famous writer, nature's lover and friend of Kumaun, Jim Corbett.

The park lies between 20^0 25' to 29^0 38'20" north, and 78^0 45' to 79^0 5' east and covers an area of 520.82 sq. km. Almost two-third

(329.98 sq km) area of the park lies in Garhwal (Pauri) and the rest (190.84 sq km) in Nainital district of Kumaun. The altitude varies from 400 to 1210 m. A parallel ridge lies from the north to the south. The highest point in the park is Kanda (1,210 m). The river Ramganga enters the park near Gairal and flows towards the west up to Sarapduli. Having a bend near Dhikala, it ultimately changes its way to the southwest for coming out of the park from Kalagarh.

Table 3.3 will indicate the climatic conditions of the park. The trend of the tourist traffic is governed by such conditions.

TABLE 3.3 : Climatic condition of the Jim Corbett National Park

Months	Temperature in C		Rainfall	Tourist in 1993	
	Maximum	Minimum	(in mm)	Number	Percentage
January	25	3	44.7	1,405	7.80
February	28	5	28.3	1,627	9.80
March	34	9	28.0	2,498	13.86
April	40	13	8.5	2,747	15.23
May	43	19	21.0	3,054	16.93
June	44	22	123.1	2,395	13.28
July	38	23	398.7	83	0.46
August	34	23	469.6	21	0.12
September	34	20	228.1	77	0.43
October	33	15	45.4	134	0.74
November	30	8	3.9	1,358	7.53
December	27	4	12.9	2,629	14.58

Source : Climate data from Ramganga Hydel Project office, Kalagarh; and tourist information from Jim Corbett National Park office, Dhikala.

In the national park, a broad flat valley known as Patalidum is the most picturesque having almost all types of flora of foothill Himalaya. Tall waving grass and feeding ground of the herbivores are mainly found here. Natural occupancy of wildlife in their carefree majesty is most fascinating view of the park. Almost all sorts of wildlife exist here. Considering the climatic conditions and visibility. November and December are the ideal months . March and April months are also busy for tourists. Table 3.4 shows the months to visit the park for watching wildlife.

TABLE 3.4: Visibility of wildlife in the Jim Corbett National Park

Months	Animals	Weather	Visibility aspects
November	Tiger, Crocodile	Cool	Poor visibility
December	As above	Cold	As above
January	As above	Cold	Improved visibility
February	Carnivores, deer, crocodile	Pleasant cool days with cold nights	As above
March	Almost all kinds of wildlife.	Nice and pleasant	As above
April	As above	As above	Improved visibility
May	As above	Compara-tively hot days	Improved visibility but dusty days

Source : Research Officer, Project Tiger, Corbett National Park ,Ramnagar.

In this park, the monkey and langur and herds of spotted deer can easily be seen, while hog deer, barking deer, *goral nilgai*, *sambar* can be seen with a little effort. The tiger and leopard certainly take the test of patience of the tourists and observation of scuffing wild bear is quite difficult. It is only sheer luck to come across a leopard-cat. Similarly, wild-cat, wild dog, jackal and others can be visible only by chance. Malani and Bijrani have provided the opportunities to observe of elephants little often. The reservoir of Ramganga Hydel Project may help those who are interested in observing *gharials* and muggers. Unique flocks of various birds patronize the lake with the main species of stroke, ducks, teals, ibises, gulls, darters, geese, sterlings and minivets.

TABLE 3.5 : Accommodation in Jim Corbett National Park

Place	Type of Accommodation	Bed capacity
1. Dhikala	Old Forest Rest House	10
	Annexes (Cabin no. 3)	14
	Suits no. A & B	4
	Cabin no. 1 & 4	12
	New Forest Rest House	8
	Hutment (3 bedded)	15
	Swiss Cottage Tents (2 bedded)	12
	Green hut	4
	Log Hut 3-tier (General and Student)	24
	TOTAL CAPACITY	103
2. Khinanauli	Forest Rest House	6
3. Sarpuli	Forest Rest House	4
4. Gairal	Old Forest Rest House	4
	New Forest Rest House	8
	TOTAL CAPACITY	12
5. Bijrani	Forest Rest House (Double bedded)	8
	Forest Rest House (Single bedded)	2
	TOTAL CAPACITY	10
6. Sultan	Forest Rest House	4
7. Kanda	Forest Rest House	4
8. Malani	Forest Rest House	4
9. Jhirna	Forest Rest House	4
TOTAL		151

Source : 1. Chief Wildlife Warden, U.P., Lucknow.
2. Tourist office, U.P. Government, New Delhi.
3. Field Director of Wildlife, Project Tiger, Ramnagar.

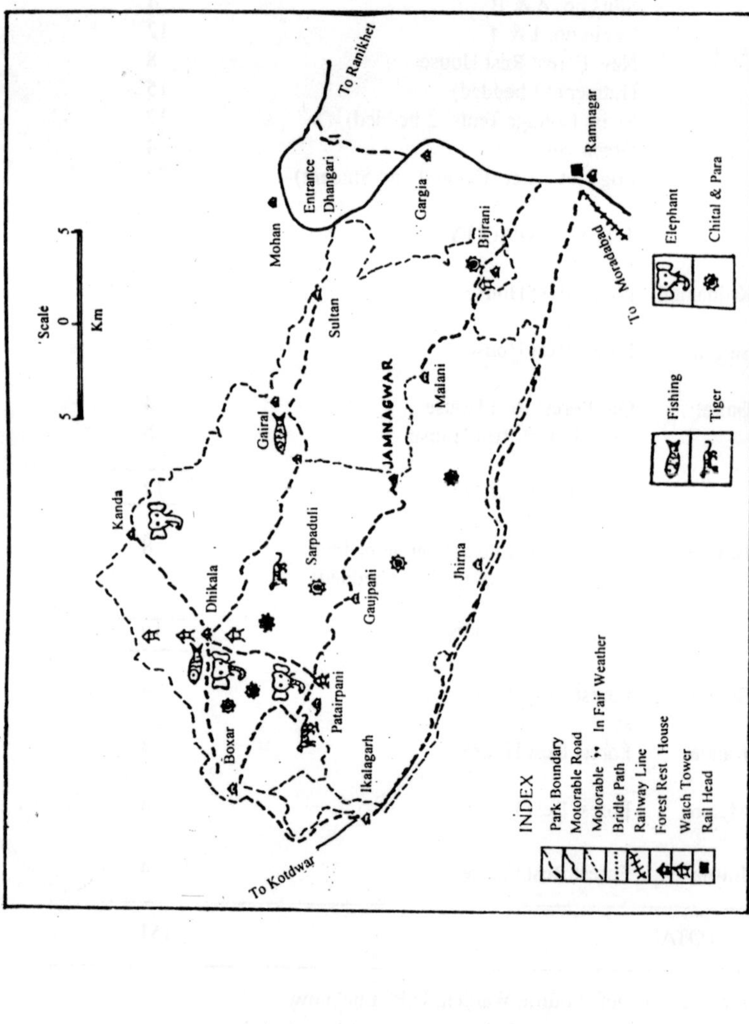

FIG. 3.7 : Guide Map of Jim Corbett National Park

Mandal, Sarpuduli, Gairal, Boxer and Dhikala are important bank of the anglers. The basking of crocodile are often observed on the river bank.

Glimpses of wild animals and birds with their natural hunts can be viewed and photographed from watch towers erected in the park. At various places in the park, such as Sarpduli, Gairal and Bijrani, accommodation and catering facilities for visitors are available. Further, Dhikala specially offers almost all possible facilities magnificent view of Ramganga with its surroundings. Internal facilities, such as catering, minibus, jeep and pick-ups are also available at various points in the park. There arc good chances for having better views of wildlife by riding elephants provided by the park authorities. Traffic guides are also provided by them as well. Medical, bank and postal services are available at Ramnagar and Kalagarh while tourist information can be collected from Dhikala. (Table 3.5).

The park is well connected by road with Delhi, Moradabad, Bareilly, Pilibhit, Lucknow, Ramnagar, Ranikhet. Dhangari is at the entrance of the Moradabad-Ranikhet road. The nearest rail head is Ramnagar situated at a distance of 51 km from this place (Fig.3.7). The park has almost fair weather roads which are negotiable only from November to June. It remains closed for tourists from mid-June to mid-September due to heavy rains and hot weather conditions. This is the worst period for tourists.

Ranikhet

Ranikhet (29^0 50' N and 79^0 25' E) is an ideal place for holidays in the region. The existence of the town dates back to 1869. Same year cantonment was established. It was selected as the most suitable place for the estates of the Britishers. A portion of the Sadar Bazaar was built by Captain R.H.W. Tromp and is still in the possession of his family and is known as Troupganj. In 1870 log huts were put up in Ranikhet for the accommodation of the troops and the First Royal Scouts and a detachment of the 37th Hampshire Regiment were sent for constructing the roads and clearing and levelling the sites for the barracks. Previous to this detachment, the British King's own 25th Scottish Borderer were sent to Seoni, as it was then intended to make a cantonment there as well, but this idea was abandoned later.

Lord Mayo, the then Governor General of British India, spent some days at Ranikhet and with Chaubatia he had a survey carried out for a line of railway from Ramnagar. The scheme was then pronounced quite feasible, and had Lord Mayo lived longer, the summer seat of the British Government of India would have been different from Shimla.

There are two stories for the derivation of the name of this town. One is that some *rani* encamped and subsequently selected the place where the club now stands. Thereby, the place was named Ranikhet or queen's field. The other story suggests that this place was a scene of many battles and the present name is corrupted version of *Ranakshetra*, i.e. field of battles.

The oldest house in the Cantonment is a bungalow which is now the residential quarters of the sub-divisional officer. The Officer Mess at Chaubatia was originally named Glenrannok and was the property of the Tromp family, as also were Holm Farm and Holm Cottage. The first shop for the European goods was by Messrs Rustomji & Sons who came to this town in 1876.

Ranikhet lies on a ridge at 1,829 m above the mean sea level and covers an area of 21.76 sq km. Its population is about 22 thousand. The importance of this resort was enhanced greatly for having a wonderful view of snowy Himalayan peaks from here. The following peaks from the west to east of the Himalayan range can be seen from Ranikhet and Chaubatia (Table 3.6)

TABLE 3.6 : Views of Snowy Himalayan Peaks from Ranikhet

Name of the peak	Height in metres
Bandarpunch	6,219
Jaunil	6,535
Bareakhanta (2 peaks)	6,478 & 6,853
Kharchakund	6,536
Badrinath and Chaukhunta	6,719
Kimatung	6,368
Nanlikhanta	6,514
Kamet of Tibet border	7,633
Mana	7,159
Rataban	6,642
Trisul	7,022
Dunagiri	6,955
East Trishul	6,708
Nandadevi	7,698
Nandakot	6,759
Panch Chuli	6,798
Tilkot	6,334
Nampa in Nepal	7,006

The township lies in between the forests mainly of *chir*, pine *banj* (oak) and cypress trees willow and older herbs are common in moist and damp situations. Deodars, chestnuts and horse chestnuts are not indigenous to Ranikhet. This delightful healthy atmosphere always captivates the tourists. All roads inside the town are well maintained and are neat and clean. The spectacle breathing in the orchards and jungles with smooth viewing of gentle sloppy terraced fields is quite enchanting.

After independence, it is functioning as the headquarters of Kumaun Regiment. Now it is also a good health and tourist resort of the region. The demand of accommodation is met by various hotels, inspection bungalows and private lodges. With the increasing tourist attractions in Ranikhet, more facilities are required.

The Chaubatia fruit orchard is a natural attraction of the tourists. Almost all tourists visiting Ranikhet make a trip to this place. It is situated at a distance of 10 km from Ranikhet bus station and at an elevation of 2,116 m above the mean sea level. It is also open to visitors for enjoying the panorama of fruit laden trees there. Fresh fruits can also be purchased during the season. Amusements varies in order to suit all types of tourists.

Ranikhet has many facilities for games. There is no other golf course of this type in the region. Temples of archaeological importance and Kumauni colourful culture attract the tourists the most.

There is a network of good motorable roads connecting Ranikhet with Almora (50 km), Nainital (59 km), Bareilly (190 km), Delhi (361 km), Ranikhet-Gopeshwar (via Karanprayag 145 km), Kausani (62 km), Pithoragarh (169 km), Bageshwar (145 km), Ramnagar (95 km), Dwarahat (39 km) and the nearest rail head at Kathgodam (84 km). Private taxis and bus services are also available here.

Tourists can have the pleasure of viewing snowy Himalayan peaks, breathful air of green forests and attractive tidiness of nature. There are a number of vintage points with nice panorama of nature. Within comparatively short distance, one can visit various places of tourist interest (Fig. 3.8 and Table 3.7).

TABLE : 3.7 : Places of Tourist Interest in and around Ranikhet

Places	Distance (km)	Special features	Approach
Chaubatia	10	Government fruit gardens and research centre, fascinating view of Himalaya	Regular bus service
Bhaludam	13	Artificial lake close to Chaubatia (3 km)	Regular bus service
Upat and Kalika	6	Upat is best mountain golf course (9 holes) and Kalika has temple and forest nursery nearby.	Motor
Majhkhali	13	Close view of snowy heights	Motor
Cooperative Drug Factory	3	Production of Ayurvedic drugs from local medicinal herbs	Motor
Tarikhet	8	A kuti of Gandhiji	Motor
Jhuladevi	5	Water reservoir and temple	Motor
Nagpapi	10	Picturesque beauty of nature and water works	Bridle path
Dwarahat	38	Cluster of old temples and principal seat of Katyuri kings. En route to Badrinath	Motor
Dunagiri	52	An ancient temple of Goddess Durga and small waterfall	Motor and Bridle path

Contd.

Table 3.7 (*Contd.*)

Places	Distance (km)	Special features	Approach
Sitlakhet	26	Charming view of snow and ideal place for peaceful holidays	As above
Khairna	22	Famous for fishing	Motor
Manila	66	Beautiful place with charming backdrop of snow clad mountain	Motor and bridle path
Pandu Kholi	55	Cluster of age old caves of Pandavas time, fascinating view with archaeological and religious importance	As above

Source : Field work by the authors.

Kausani

Kausani is the most favourable tourist centre in the interior of the region. Enchanting snowy views can never be forgotten. The unique agricultural valley of Garur enhances the importance. It is claimed that Kausani has been the worship place of Kaushik Muni, perhaps from which it derived its name. However, there are no evidences to support this claim.

This town is famous for sun rise and sun set. An increasing number of tourists and businessmen are contributing towards its prosperity. It also helps in sharing the pressure of tourists in Nainital during the peak season. In 1929, the Father of the Nation, Gandhiji, came here and had stayed for 12 days. During that period he wrote a commentary on *Gita*, known as *Anashakti Yoga.* He highly praised the natural beauty and gave the name "Indian Switzerland" to this resort. Sarla Ben, a disciple of Gandhiji, established an Ashram here in 1947. She originally came from the United States and

A. Panoramic view of Almora township

B. Ranikhet township alongwith its Sylvan environs

PLATE – V

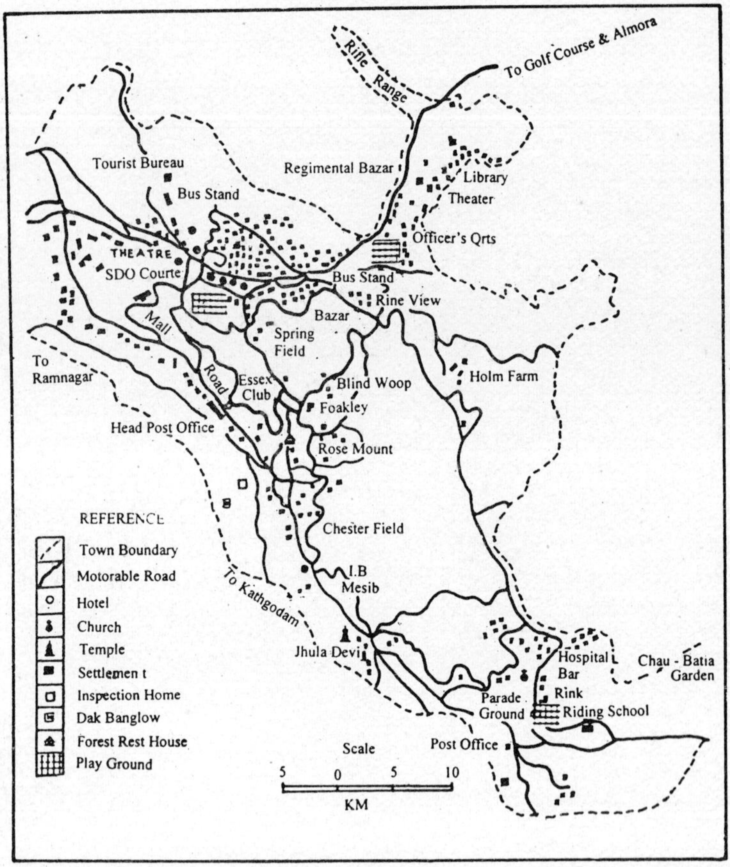

FIG. 3.8 : Ranikhet

was earlier known as Katherine Marry Herlme. Since 1964 Anashakti Ashram is run by other disciples of Gandhiji.

Kausani lies at an height of 1,890 m above the mean sea level, and en route to Almora-Bageshwar motor road. It is situated at a distance of 52 km from Almora, 40 km from Bageshwar and 74 km from Ranikhet. Due to these connections, this beauty spot became popular resort. It provides natural freshness to all sorts of tourists. It is influenced by the northern and southern parts of Kumaun. With the development of education, electricity and

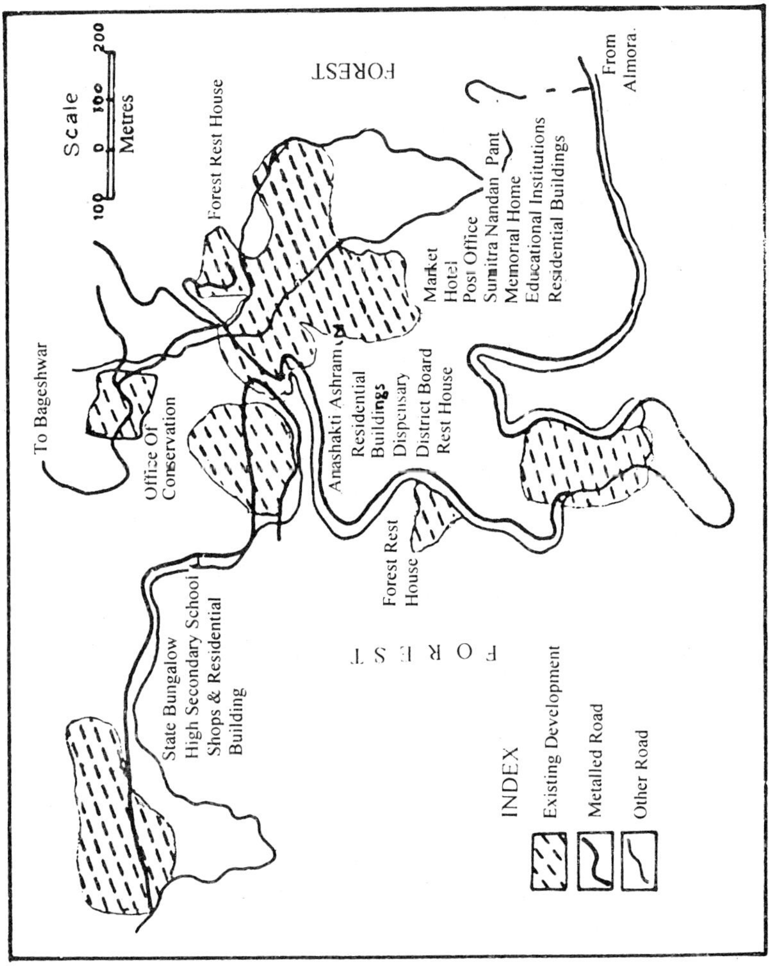

Fig. 3.9 : Kausani

A. Bird's Eye-View of Bhowali

B. Picturesque Bhimtal with an island inside the lake

PLATE – VI

water facilities, the improvement in the number and quality of buildings is also apparent. An army unit has been constituted here. The progress of this centre is likely to be improved further (Fig 3.9).

Tourists from India and abroad visit this place, but tourists from Uttar Pradesh, West Bengal, Maharashtra, Delhi, Gujarat and Rajasthan are large in number. Foreign tourists are comparatively few. A good number of tourists come by conducted tours from Nainital and only a few tourists stay a night here.

Bhimtal

Bhimtal (29^0 21' N and 79^0 84' E), is situated at an altitude of 1,372 m, is most picturesque and attractive tourist resort of Kumaun. Like every hill station in the Himalayan region, it has its own peculiar captivating charms. Bhimtal has a lake enclosed by lush green fields, and is largest lake of this region. Bhimtal lake has a small island in the centre with almost all expected facilities of bar, restaurant and catering facilities. Island is decorated with flowers, airy shed and benches, which enhances the beauty of the lake. This island can be approached by rowing boats.

There is a masonry dam close to colourful terraced garden with flowing canals. An old temple of Bhim built by Raja Baj Bahadur Chand in seventeenth century A.D. is also nearby the dam. The town derives its name from this temple.

The outstanding attractions are fishing, boating and hunting. There is a small market to cater to the essential needs of the tourists. Bhimtal is ideal spot for conducting tour from Nainital. There are a number of picnic points providing the excellent sites for hiking as well. Nainital is 22.5 km and Kathgodam 20 km (nearest rail head) away from this place.

TABLE 3.8 : Places of tourist interest in and around Bhimtal

Place	Distance (km)	Special features	Approach
Lake island		Natural island view	Boat
Naukuchiatal	4	Flourishing of lotus flower in the lake. A place for fishing and migratory birds.	Bus
Sat Tal	5	A captivating picturesque spot where nature reigns supreme. An ashram is also situated.	Jeep
Malwatal	4	Small hunting, fishing in the lake and natural viewing of wild deer and Ghurar.	Bridle

Source : Field work by the authors.

Bhowali

Bhowali boasts of an excellent climatic conditions. It is a health resort at an height of 1,707 m above the mean sea level. Fresh air comes through the surrounding slopes densely covered by forests of oak and pine. This fresh air gives life and energy to the living being. There is a sanatorium for the patients of tuberculosis in the town. (Fig. 3.10).

The fruit market is full almost the year round. Apples, plums, pears, peaches, apricot and so many variety of temperate climatic fruits are sent from here to different places in the country. Other attractions for tourists is fish hatching centre. There are a few hotels with a small market for catering and lodging needs of the tourists and local visitors.

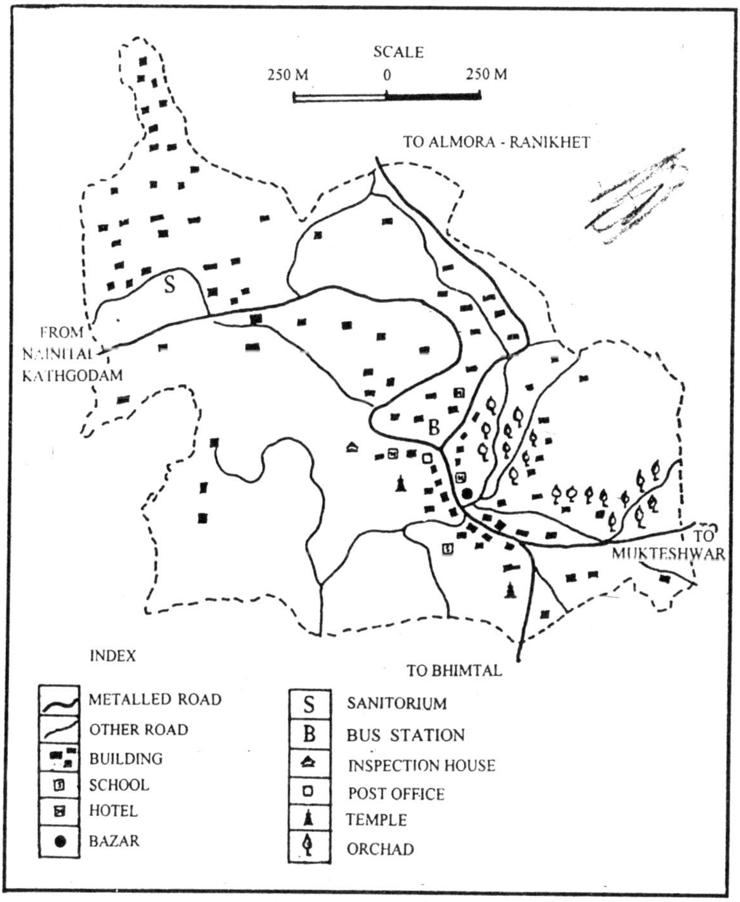

FIG. 3.10 : Bhowali

Bhowali lies on both sides of the road routes leading to Almora, Ranikhet, Ramgarh, Mukteshwar, Nainital, Haldwani and Bhimtal with distances of 32 km, 45 km, 10 km, 11 km, 48 km and 6 km respectively. Ghorakhal, 3 km away from Bhowali, is a centre having a temple and Sainik school and is also a beautiful place for the tourists (Table 3.8).

Garur-Baijnath

Baijnath village lying at an elevation of approximately 1,000m above mean sea level is well-known for its archaeological, historical and religious background with natural hill and valley attractions. Baijnath is situated at the confluence of rivers Gomati and Garur-Ganga rivulets. Garur-Baijnath valley is interesting as being the centre of Katuries who were the first rulers of Kumaun's of historical significance. The present art, architecture and culture enriched during the period of the Katurian kings was followed and enriched by the Chand dynasty. This place has also accrued medicinal property of herbs and plants.

The chronology concerning the temples is well known. It is believed that the style of workmanship displayed on these temples assigns them approximately to fourteenth century A.D. It is also claimed that degenerated variety of late Salanki-Vaghela architecture was received from Gujarat and Rajputana in fifteenth century A.D. hence the architecture of Kumaun has been fascinating. After all it can not be denied that the Hindu architecture in Kumaun remained highly significant up to fifteenth and sixteenth century A.D. (after Gupta period). The credit of building a major portion of these temples and sculptures of aesthetic sense goes to the Katurian rulers. Following this, Chand further developed the art and architecture of this region.

The principal deities at Baijnath temple complex are the Rakshasa Deoi, Laxmi Narayan, Nritya Ganapati, Karttikeya, Narsimha, Brahma, Parvati, Mahisasurmardini, Sapta Natrikas, Surya, Garuda and Kubera. They reflect several complexities of political conditions as well as religious recognition and traditions.

Garur-Baijnath is also an agricultural area of Kumaun. It is full of orchards, agricultural fields and gardens. Valuable archaeological treasure with enchanting natural beauty, medicinal

A. Jageshwar temple complex (Almora)

B. 'Sun Temple' cluster of Katarnal (Almora)

PLATE – VII

herbs and plants, attractive folk art, and colourful culture and customs are seen here. With the improvement of transportation and communication and facilities for accommodation, catering, market, hospital, bank and the like, this resort will become an ideal centre for tourism in the region. Uttar Pradesh Tourism Department has to pay attention for its rapid development and advertisement by all possible means of publicity.

Baijnath is a pilgrimage centre of the region and provides very good means for hiking and trekking adventures. Pilgrims arrive here on the occasion of Shivaratri and Sankranti festivals while for other tourists it is always open throughout the year. However, the flow is more during the summer and autumn seasons, which of course is linked with the visits to other hill resorts of Kumaun, such as Nainital, Almora, Ranikhet and Kausani.

Baijnath is 131 km away from Nainital and 65 km from Almora. But no proper transport facilities are available for this place. There is no direct bus service up to Baijnath from Nainital, and even from Almora. There are a few bus routes touching this place, such as Ranikhet-Bageshwar, and Moradabad-Gwaldam (UPSRTC). KMOU Bus Service are from Nainital to Bageshwar, Gwaldam to Haldwani, Haldwani to Thal, Haldwani to Kapkot; and frequent bus services are available from Almora beyond Baijnath. All these bus services run through this town. In spite of all above services, there is a lack of transportational facilities because almost all buses are overcrowded and with least punctuality. Baijnath is only 12 km from Kausani but the conduct tour operators generally do not include Baijnath in their programme. Being the centre of architectural excellence of Kumaun, this centre needs more facilities to become a true resort in true sense. Baijnath and Garur are closely connected with each other as they are within a kilometre distance.

Bageshwar

Bageshwar (29 50' N and 79 46' E) is a historical and religious town situated at the confluence of the river Gomati and Saryu and on en-route to the famous Pindari glacier. Being rich in ancient shrines, it is famous for its annual fair of Uttarayani of great commercial importance which is held in the month of January every year.

Though situated in the wide valley, Bageshwar is 975 m above the mean sea level. The name is derived from the ancient temple of Lord Bagnath (Shiva). The temple was established by Raja Laxmi Chand in about 1450 A.D. Within a group of 15 shrines, it is included as a pilgrim centre. The age old temple of Bagnath, Bhairavnath and Datternath attracts thousands of devotees every year specially on the occasion of Uttarayani fair when the tourists can enjoy the cultural life of Kumaun. The fair is used to be a great mart of exchange of Tibetan products between the Bhotiyas and the merchants from Almora and surroundings (Atkinson, 1973).

Bageshwar provides comfortable accommodation in the Tourist Home, Dak Bungalow and in several hotels. The resort is now developing as a tourist centre in the region. This town is well connected with regular bus service from Almora, Baijnath, Nainital and Ranikhet. It has a number of tourist centres in its neighbouring areas and most of them are of religious significance.

Ramgarh

Located in the high peaks of the Gagar range at a height of 2,280 m above the mean sea level, Ramgarh is full of orchards of apple, plum, peaches and apricot which makes Ramgarh extremely beautiful during summers. A fruit preservation factory under the administration of the Director of Fruit Utilisation of the Government of Uttar Pradesh is located here. Besides fruits, a new venture of

A Historic Remnant of Chand Dynesty – A Guesardeval temple. Dwarahat, (Almora)

PLATE – VIII

production of flowers (*glydolla*) has successfully been launched here which has proved to be commercially viable as well.

Ramgarh derives its name from a small Ramgarh river which flows through this settlement. This place is famous due to different reasons. It is the summer resort of great poetess Mahadevi Verma. Gurudev Ravindranath Tagore completed a large part of his famous *Gitanjali* at a cottage here, now known as Tagore Top. It was also a working place of great Narayan Swami. An intermediate college has been established in his memory. At Talla Ramgarh, a branch of Pondicherry Ashram is also located. The ruins of a village Nayak, which was famous for its beauty and dance, are at Talla Ramgarh.

Its natural and pleasant views attract many tourists. In spite of its captivating natural landscape, Ramgarh cannot provide comfort to its tourists because only a single dak bungalow and a few tea stalls exist there. However, bus services are available at Talla and Malla Ramgarh. U.P. Hortico is situated at the latter place. Ramgarh may be benefited by the recent government's policy to develop new tourist centres.

Mukteshwar

Mukteshwar (29^0 28' N and 79^0 40' E) is situated at an elevation of 2,275 to 2,346 m above the mean sea level and lies on the crest of hill of Kumaun where the Gargachal and Lohukot ranges meet. Deep valley of Ramgarh lies on one side of this beauty spot, while on the other side, the hill range go down to Bhabar.

A splendid view of snow clad Himalaya is visible from here. In the ancient period it was famous due to the Mahadeo temple. At present, it is famous for the Indian Veterinary Research Institute (IVRI) which was established in 1893 during the British period. In 1901, a meteorological station was established here. After independence, sub-station of the Central Potato Research Institute was also located here (Fig. 3.11).

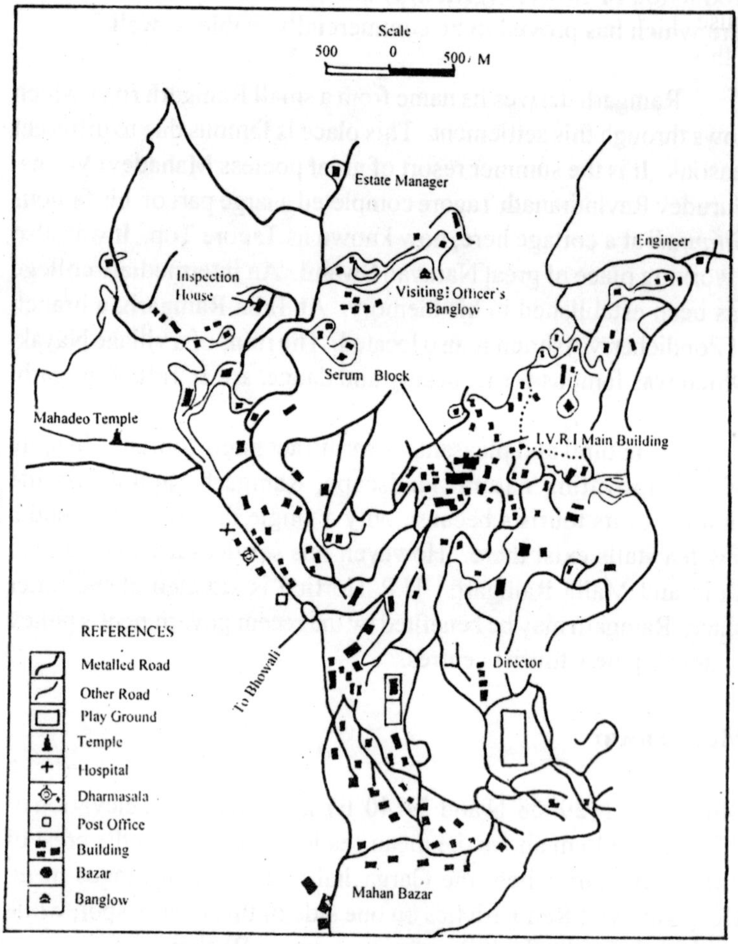

FIG. 3.11 : Mukteshwar

Glimpses of Rudrapur, Baijpur, Kashipur and distant views of Almora and Ramgarh can easily be seen from here specially at night when the sky is clear.

Orchards around Mukteshwar are famous. Therefore, it became a favourite tourist resort of the region. Only an inspection house is available for comfortable stay of the tourists. Short visit to this fascinating hill station is recommended. The surrounding area is now developing as an apple belt of the region.

In addition to the above there are numerous small centres of some significance. These places are under explored. Nevertheless, once their importance is realized, the tourists map of this region is likely to be changed. The region has great potentialities. With better transportational facilities and publicity, the economy of the region can be transformed to a great extent.

REFERENCES

Anonymous (1913), *Handbook and Dictionary of Ranikhet Cantonment*, Pio-neer Press, Allahabad.

Atkinson, E.T. (1973), *The Himalayan Gazetteer*, Vol. III, Part II,Cosmos Publications, Delhi (Reprinted).

Atkinson, E.T. (1982-84), *The Himalayan Districts of Northwestern Provinces of India*, Vol. XI, Cosmos Publication (Reprinted)

Kaur, J. (1985), *Himalayan Pilgrimages and New Towns*, Himalayan Books, New Delhi.

Jha, M. (ed) (1985), *Dimensions of Pilgrimage*, Inter-India Publications, New Delhi.

Nag, P. and S. Sengupta (1992), *Geography of India,* Concept Publishing Company, New Delhi (Chapter 21; Places of Tourist, Historical and Cultural Importance).

Nevilli, H.R. (1904) (ed), *District Gazetteer, Nainital.*

NATMO (1989), *Tourist Atlas of India*, National Atlas & Thematic Mapping Organisation, Calcutta.

NATMO (1985), *Glimpses of India*, National Atlas & Thematic Mapping Organisation, Calcutta.

Chapter 4

SOCIO-ECONOMIC AND CULTURAL DIMENSIONS

India is not merely a nation in political or conventional context, but it is a conglomeration of castes, customs and cultures, races and religions, fairs and festivals. These features are also well represented in the region. The whole range of activities revolve around the people, and movement of people generates tourism. For this purpose, all the cultural activities of tourist attraction should be promoted in order to continue the folk and other traditional glories. Thus, culture, fairs and festivals become important for the tourists as well as for the inhabitants of the region.

People from different sections of physio-ecological settings have different customs and expressions of the life, culture and related aspects. They have different perception, dresses, habits of eating and even way of expression, and such variations are worth observing for the tourists, for example during Dussehra people from different castes and customs take part in enjoying the functions, ballet and raising effigy (*putla*). This activity which had been limited to a particular section of the society till yesterday is now being accepted by everyone thereby breaking almost all traditional barriers of differentiations. Such transformations are noticed during the Ramleela, Dussehra, Nandadevi fair, Uttarayani and Basant Panchimi. Further, tourists and local inhabitants are continuously exposed to each other. The latter prepare various products and sell them for their livelihood. Tourists purchase these items which help them to strengthen the economy of the region. The places of cultural interest for the tourists are shown in Fig. 4.1.

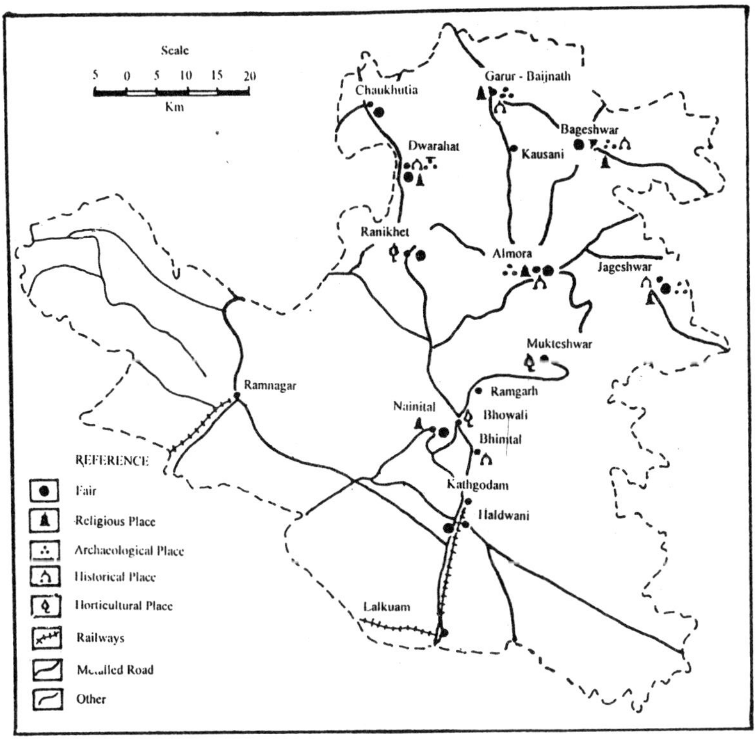

FIG. 4.1 : Nainital Region : Places of Socio-cultural Interest

Social Background

Since very ancient time social gatherings have been an important feature for movement. People do assemble for cheering up and religious worship on the occasions of fairs and festivals. This region has prominent traditional characteristics, however there is increasing influence of westernization and modern growth. The religious functions have their social, cultural and economic impacts as well. There is no environmental pollution *per se* but intoxication, inebriation and hippie culture have been increasing.

There has been a change in cultural traditions from the ancient times which can easily be traced in the society of Kumaun. The traditional Kumaun society had the congruence between economic and social stratification through *Jajmani* system, which has brought greater stability and relative freedom. Therefore, much of the social conflicts and political trifle remain confined to the top strata of the social pyramid and hardly ever effect the whole Kumaun society. The predominance of economy had sustained the freedom of the individual, integrated the community, and maintained the structure of family as a broader unit of social, economic and cultural entity. People have faith in traditional Hindu world, view of predestination, *Karma*, *Dharma* and *Moksha.* The role of faith was notable in the motivational aspects of human behaviour due to which percept and practice usually went together unlike in modern times. In social system based on faith, the differences between the theory and practice are minimum, but when faith weakens and gives way to rationality, the very consideration of the rationality criteria itself makes the practice of percepts difficult.

This leads us to the role of elites and intellectuals as preservers of the norms of society. According to the traditional structure, there was little scope for social circulation of elites (Tripathi, 1983). For maintaining of old age Kumaun traditional structure, no modernization is needed to disturb the ancient rhythmic, vibration and harmony of the region.

Nainital region has been dominated by the Kumaunies and Khas Rajpoots. The Brahmins are the later edition of Mongoloid and Caucasoid races. Temperate zone (1,200-2,400 m above sea level) is the homeland of Khasas with the conformity of climate they are distinguished by their cuts, tall features, fair in complexion and shape of nose. Now absorbed with the subsequent group of the migrated population of Brahmins of plains but yet a few distinctions of this group is also found in the inner valleys of the region. In any case, the valleys of this region have given almost all opportunties to human habitations, therefore this area became one of the early settled part of the country; while Bhabar zone was refused by the people due to unhealthy climatic conditions (Tiwari and Singh, 1983).

Employment

As a result of tourist activity, a large number of workers are able to seek employment in this region. The effect of tourism, both in employment and income is quite apparent. The goods and services require financial support. It does not affect only the income from tourism, but also employment as transport workers and their operators, local agents, hotel and restaurant owners, hotel guides, waiters, cooks and local agents and many others who are directly or indirectly related to such activities. Further, employment becomes possible for skilled and unskilled people by the tourism and such income can develop backward areas of the region which has limited source of alternative employment, as is often so, in the case of non-industrial areas deficient in natural resources other than scenic attractions and climate (Robinson, 1976).

In Nainital region much people are considerably affected by heavy tourist influence. At present about 1,300 people in this region are engaged in different services, i.e. rickshaw pullers, porters, boat peddlers and the like. In addition, Almora, Ranikhet, Kausani and other tourist resorts have also got seasonal job opportunities for a large number of people. On the basis of survey, it is estimated that about 5,000 persons are engaged in various hotels, lodges, boarding, cafe and restaurant.

The spirit of adventure, and the inquisitiveness for discovering and exploration has promoted tourism since the dawn of civilization. Nowadays the spirit of adventure and underlying risks remain but means of travel have become easier. However, industry in this region is still in need of proper attention and it can prove to be a blessing in disguise. Besides providing job opportunities to the local people it always draws the attention of conservationists to protect the natural resources.

Cultural Aspects

The traditional sources of entertainment have been fairs and festivals which are some of the occasions of social assembly, while public worship are basically religious in outlook. They have their socio-cultural and economic significance as well. A number of fairs and festivals are celebrated in the region but some of them are more exceptional and important. The Nandadevi fair celebrated in the month of August-September in the honour of goddess by the same name who represents goddess *Parwati*. It is best celebrated in Nainital, Ranikhet and Almora with colourful traditional costumes and folk music. The beating of *hurka* drum with folk songs and dances (locally known as *Jhora* and *Chanchari)* are unique and add gaiety to the atmosphere.

The Uttarayani is a religious fair held at Bageshwar and at Chitrashila (Ranibagh near Haldwani), when the sun rays start to lose their slanting towards the northern hemisphere in the month of January. This fair is celebrated in the study region and is also locally known as *Ghughitia.*

In the study region every festival has its importance. The main local festivals are *Haryala, Khatarwa, Phooldeli, Bhitoli, Ghee-sankranti* etc. All these activities are related to the cultural cycle. Besides these, there are numerous local fairs in various places of the region. The major Muslim festivals are also celebrated in the region as well. Id-ul-Zuha or Bakr-id (famous for animal sacrifice), Muharram (period of mourning), Ramzan (month of fasting) and Id-ul-Fitr are quite significant. Buddha Jayanti is celebrated by the worshippers of Buddha in the month of May

An Archetectural monument – Maha Mritunjaya temple, Jageshwar, (Almora)

PLATE IX

particularly in Nainital. Further, the Sikh celebrate the birthday of Guru Nanak ji and Guru Govind Singh by reciting Guru Granth Sahib with great interest. The *gurudwara* is the main centre of such activities. The important *gurudwaras* are situated in Nainital, Haldwani, Ramnagar and Bageshwar. However, the region is dominated by Hindus. Most of the historical and cultural monuments are naturally linked with the Hindu tradition and faith. In the ancient period, several rulers built temples on the hill slopes having peace and silence which may occasionally be disturbed by the various wild animals and birds. There are a number of temples spread all over the region but a few of them are worth visiting, such as Nandadevi at Nainital, Bagnath at Bageshwar, Jagnath at Jageshwar, Gananath at Takula, Kalika at Ranikhet, Kapileshwar at Mukteshwar, Bhimeshwar at Bhimtal, Chital and Syahidevi at Almora. Some of them are the centres for fairs and ceremonial gatherings.

The region has rich cultural heritage which comprises archaeological, historical and scenic places of national significance. All these places have maintained the local history for a long time. Many tourists keep on visiting these places year after year. The rajas ruled over various parts of the region, built many temples on the hill tops, at the confluence of the rivers and in the lap of valleys.

The Katyuris who were the first historic rulers of Kumaun, had a high aesthetic sense so the credit of building major portions of the temples and associated sculptures goes to them. Following this, the Chand dynasty ruled Kumaun from the plains and influenced the art and architecture of the region. But the most remarkable period, which has left deeper marks on the architecture begins after the eleventh century A.D. The temples after this period more or less were on the Pratihara style.

The region has a great potentiality for attracting more tourists from the country and abroad if the archaeological and historical sites are properly managed and publicised.

The Impact of Tourism on Culture

The fairs and festivals of this region are basically religious in nature, and very good source of entertainment and recreation. They present colourful picture of the Kamauni culture. Those who participate in these activities infuse a lot of happiness, relaxation and joy–far away from the hard, dull, stressful and strained daily routine.

Tourism brings social changes through higher standards of living alongwith increase in leisure and quick and soft means of transportation. Peters has remarked that tourism creates social benefits from widening of people's interests generally in world affairs and to a new understanding of foreigners and foreign tastes (Peters, 1969). The World Council of Churches has underlined the negative aspects of tourism. According to this body, "An excessive number of tourists can generate social strains in small and unsophisticated communities. The human effect, on this scale and international scale of competition for tourist consumers has been given too little attention and deserves serious research.

Cultural tourism (visiting fairs, temples, historical sites etc.) plays a significant role in strengthening regional, national and international goodwill and understanding as well. It obviously means that such activities bring the people of different nationalities, diversified cultural background, varied social values, castes and customs come closer.

Group folk-dance and songs are very common during fairs and festivals which presents a reflection of the cultural heritage. For enjoyment, men and women of the region dance and sing together. They are musicians by birth and dance come naturally out of them. They express their joys and sorrows, bravery, orthodoxy, domestic affairs and beauty through various ways and methods according to local faith and belief.

A. *Jhora* (a folk) dancing women in their colourful robes

B. Traditional folk *Chholia* (Almora)
PLATE – X

Among the musical instruments, *Hurka* and *Bansuri* (flute) are most important one while other instruments are *Turuhi* (curved-horn), *Nagara* (trumpet), *Mushekbeen* (bagpipe) etc. The popular folk-dance and ballet are *Jhora, Chanchari, Chholia, Malushai, Hurka-Baul, Rituraina* and *Saramasi.*

Jagar is another very important tradition of the region. It has been a religious practice to worship local deities to get rid of evil spirits. Most people worshipped deity in the region is *Golla Dewata* whose temples are situated at Chitai, Ghorakhal and Gairar. In these temples, thousands of people worship every year during the time of Dussehra and sacrifice goats. Bholanath, Saim and Ganganath are other well-known local deities. The persons who play *hurka* and beat a bronze plate with two wooden sticks and recite songs of praise to invite God are known as *Jagaria* and on whom the sacred spirit of the invited God is to come are known as *Dangaria.* The latter dances in the rhythm of *hurka* and bronze plate and tells miraculous facts about the future.

At present new attitudes and traditions are being introduced. These festivals indicate the changing and developing conditions of the region. The resort town of Nainital celebrates summer and autumn festivals in the month of May and June, and October respectively. The town is decorated with multicoloured lights and buntings. A number of cultural activities, music, dances, dramas, sports and exhibitions are performed for recreation of tourists so that they may extend their visits. Nainital in particular and Almora, Ranikhet in general invite the tourists by such modern means of attractions. These festivals are organized by the Municipal Board of the concerned town. This helps in promoting tourism and also helps in changing socio-economic values of the people of interior areas.

Economic Impact

In India tourism is the fifth largest export industry which is a good source of earning foreign exchange without exporting the goods and without spoiling the natural resources or wealth (Appendix V). Tourist industry never makes losses. The success in attracting foreign tourists depends much on the capacity to publicize in the outside world. India can still earn much more foreign exchange from international tourism. By this activity, minimum damage to the local environment may be caused in comparison to other economic activities. This country must be presented as a dynamic nation with an appropriate combination of traditional and modern facets. Gigantic industrial complexes do exist here by the side of centres of ancient culture. It do offer comforts and luxuries of modern facilities of transportation, communication and accommodation. But, in spite of all its resources, India has been able to attract a few foreign tourists. The country's share from international tourism has increased from 0.17 to 0.27 per cent while earnings from tourism have increased from, 0.30 to 0.67 per cent during 1970 to 1980. The estimated tourist arrival was 800 thousand in 1980 and 1,164 thousands in 1987, while the total estimated foreign exchange earning of the country was Rs. 1,166 crore and Rs. 1,890 crore during the above period (Nag and Sengupta, 1992). Increasing leisure time, improving standard of living and cultural attitudes towards visiting new places, and ever improving means of transportation are the cause of the rapid growth of tourism all over. Expansion of education has created cultural awareness for stimulating the desire for travel (Hellen, 1966).

In the Nainital region, tourism has worked as the backbone of the regional economy. Unlike industry, tourism is much more pervasive in its economic impact, it represents an injection of external purchasing power into the economy widely distributed in its initial regional impact and acting as a stimulus to every sector of economy (Cosgrove and Jackson, 1972). A large part of total earning of the local people in the resort is determined by tourist industry either in direct or indirect way, because the economy of the resort town more of less depends upon tourism which includes different industries, e.g. activities related to transportation, accommodation, catering, recreation and the like.

In order to assess the possible economic impact, the tourists were contacted and requested to fill up a questionnaire, but such type of information do not exactly reflect the real income gained by engagement in the tourist industry. The impact of tourism in the local economy may be gathered from the organizers of the contract tour programmes. However, by the questionnaire it was possible to trace out that the large part of the expenses was on the primary needs, i.e. food and lodging and partly on recreation. Travel and shopping are the other heads of expenditure (Table 4.1).

TABLE 4.1 : Nature of expenditure (1986)

Nature of expenditure	Expenditure in %
Food, Lodging and Recreation	48.6
Travel	20.3
Shopping	18.4
Miscellaneous	12.7
Number of tourists contacted	500

Source : Field work by the authors.

Governmental and non-governmental bodies have a good source of income from tourist industry in the area. In the region, Jim Corbett National Park earns much of foreign exchange by way of entrance fees, camera fees, lodging charges, fishing licence fee, bait charges and elephants ride charges. Municipal boards earns considerable amount from the tourist industry. Their earnings in various years can be estimated on the basis of total tourist flow and rate of toll tax. Table 4.2 will indicate the earnings of the municipal boards of Nainital and Almora. The toll tax charges have been Rs. 2 for each bus passenger and Rs. 4 for the car and jeep passenger. The Table 4.2 shows an increase of the revenue by the way of toll-tax. It also reflects the flow of tourists. There has been a gradual increase in

TABLE 4.2 : Income of Nainital and Almora Municipal Boards from passenger toll tax

Year	Earnings by passenger toll tax	
	Nainital	Almora
1978	8,96,188	5,89,730
1979	9,75,422	6,41,930
1980	9,59,540	6,50,678
1981	10,25,410	6,71,578
1982	9,70,606	6,88,454
1983	9,38,734	6,99,262
1984	10,78,810	7,68,880
1985	10,91,630	7,45,020
1986	11,01,018	7,71,228
1987	N.A.	6,93,460

Source : Nainital and Almora Municipal Boards.

Nainital whereas in the case of Almora it has been fluctuating from 1984 onwards. Tourists from Nainital generally go straight to Kausani and other places avoiding Almora. This pattern of movement has been responsible for fluctuations.

REFERENCES

Cosgrove, I. and Jackson, R. (1972), *The Geography of Recreation and Leisure*, Hutchinson University Library, London.

Department of Tourism (1982), *Tourist Statistics*, Government of India, New Delhi.

Hellen, Kim, (1966), *An Educator's Evaluation of Tourism*, Report Part A, 15th Annual Conference, San Francisco, California.

Lawson, F. and Baud-Bovy, M. (1977), *Tourism and Recreation Development*, Architectural Press, London.

Nag, P. and Sengupta, S. (1992), *Geography of India*, Concept Publishing Company, New Delhi.

Peters, M. (1969), *International Tourism*, Hutchinson.

Robinson, H. (1976), *A Geography of Tourism*, Macdonald and Evans Ltd., London

Tiwari, M.M. and Singh, S.K. (1983), The urban facts of U.P. Himalaya in historical prospects, in O.P. Singh (ed), *The Himalaya : Nature, Man and Culture*, Rajesh Publications, New Delhi, pp. 291-7.

Tripathi, S. (1983), Kumaun Society – Its structure, change and social policy, in O.P Singh (ed), *The Himalaya : Nature, Man and Culture*, Rajesh Publications, New Delhi.

Chapter 5

CIVIC AMENITIES AND PUBLIC UTILITY SERVICES

Transportation and communication, accommodation facilities, electric supply and running water, sewage disposal and drainage, medical services, banking facilities, shops and other sociocultural institutions of recreation and entertainment have been responsible for the present status of the tourist industry in the region (Fig 5.1). The provision for developing the services is basically related to make the area more attractive to the visitors. Nevertheless, these facilities and services have profound impact on life style and standard of local inhabitants of the region. Therefore, the evaluation of the civic amenities and public utility services has been essential for the present study. However, the improvement of any sort makes this region more inducing to both, the local people as well as to the visitors.

Transportation and Communication

Transportation plays an important role in the movement of the short time visitors who have intention to avail trouble free visits to cover maximum number of places in a short time. The transport network is considered as the nervous system of a region, particularly which has tourist industry. Nearly all the economic activities as well as the transformation of the cultural landscape are dependent on this network.

In the region, the impact of physiography on transportation development can easily be traced. The *Bhabar* region has concentration of almost all transportational activities due to quite favourable physical environment. However, conditions are divorced within the region because physiographic conditions are not favourable for the proper development of the transport network. Therefore, the proper utilization of natural resources remains relatively less tapped.

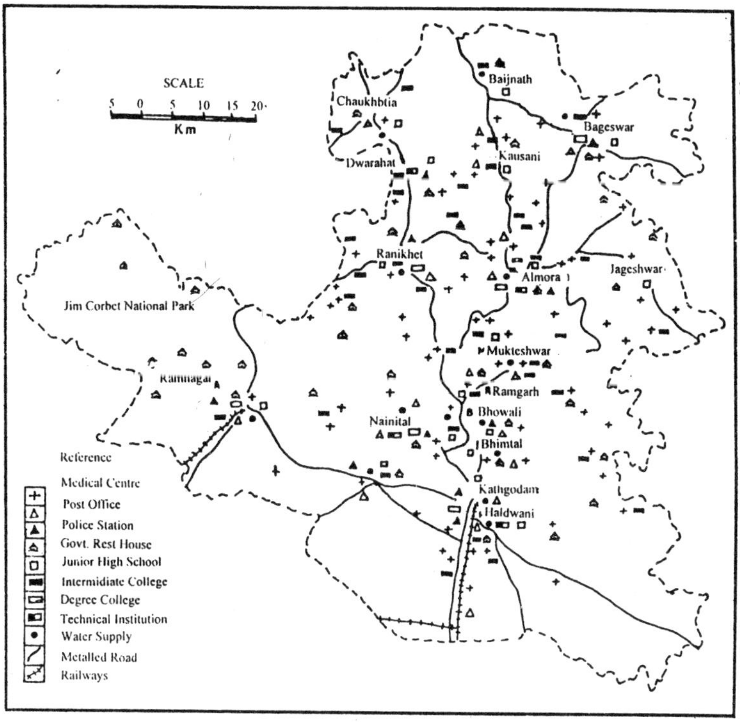

FIG. 5.1 : Nainital Region : Civic Amenities

In the early period, the transportation links developed from administrative point of view rather than economic aspects. There is no evidence available of transport network before the Chand period in this region. Maximum transportation and communication was done through river valleys in the period of the Katyuri Kings. Almost all routes along the bridle tracks were unmetalled.

During the Chand period, people from plains were attracted by fertile valleys of this region basically for agriculture. They came and permanently settled here. Due to demand and supply, the then Chand rulers felt the necessity of road construction between the valleys and places of administrative significance.

In this period, the main transportation networks were connecting the fertile valleys of River Kosi like the areas around present day Nainital, Almora, Dhikala and Ramnagar. Another linkage was Rudrapur/Ranibagh connection, while Kashipur and Ramnagar were poorly connected during the same period. The main route was through Ramnagar town but there was no *pukka* (metalled) road therefore communication was difficult during rainy season. Only carts could ply between November to June.

As mentioned earlier, after the Chand there was Gorkha period which proved to be a dark period for the development of Kumaun. In this period, construction of roads was totally based on political considerations. The existing roads were used by the inhabitants and others were unmetalled. During the British period, road construction was given some priority because they wanted to exploit the natural resources of the region. Forest roads were constructed mainly to exploit their resources. During this period also, road construction was aloof from the development of the rural economy. After independence, the transportation system was revitalized under the proper management of the Indian government. At present, transport network is satisfactory. Almost every important place has been linked by motorable roads and bridle paths (Fig. 5.2).

In this region, motor roads and railways have their impact. Roads are one of the most important factor for urbanization. They are usually developed along the river valleys. Although the roads have been constructed in the major part of the region, yet there is a further scope of development. The total length of metalled road in the area is 2,693 km (Table 5.1).

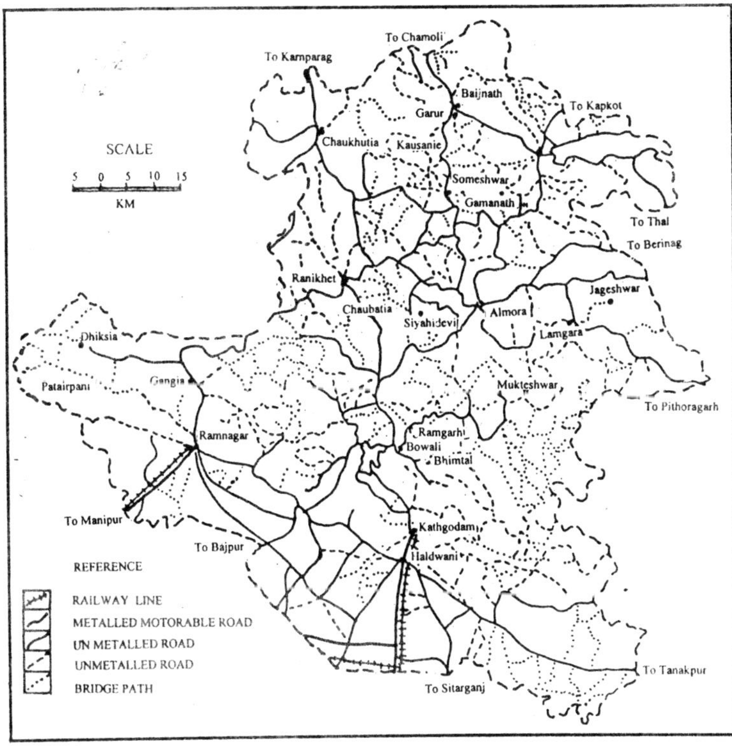

FIG. 5.2 : Transport system in Nainital Region

A new chapter in the development of the region was opened on 24th October 1884 with the introduction of railways. Railways transformed the economic activities in the rural areas of Bhabar region. Out migration of rural population was now possible. When the population pressure in the hills crossed its limits, migration to plains took place in order to find out better opportunities. In this way, a change came in the economy of the rural population. Haldwani-Kathgodam and Ramnagar became the main railheads for the region. At present this region is served by the Northern and Northeastern railways. Due to such development, this region was exposed to tourism as well. Tourists prefer to avail the railways till the farthest point and then only by roads because of safety and convenience. Further, there are air strips as well but they are ineffective.

TABLE 5.1 : Distribution of metalled roads (km)

Name of the block	Road Length
Okhalkanda	135
Betalghat	123
Ramgarh	276
Bhimtal	225
Dhari	109
Kotabagh	93
Haldwani	126
Ramnagar	184
Takula	176
Dhauladevi	192
Bhaisiachhana	88
Lumgarh	104
Hawalbagh	259
Garur	78
Bageshwar	99
Chaukhutia	67
Tarikhet	179
Dwarahat	180
TOTAL	2,693

Source : Statistical Book, 1986, Almora and Nainital.

Keeping in view the distribution of roads, it is apparent that the area of comparatively higher accessibility is found nearby the tourist destinations in the region. Haldwani, Kathgodam, Nainital, Bhowali, Bhimtal, Jim Corbett National Park are much accessible, encircling several places of tourist interest. However, Mukteshwar, Ramgarh, Jageshwar and Lumgarh are relatively in less accessible due to their location.

In view of the intra-accessibility, only flat areas are being served by the rickshaw and tempos. Nainital and Bageshwar towns do have rickshaw facilities, while in other hill destinations tourists have to move on foot. Horse and dandi are alternative to rickshaw, but they are not easily available. In Nainital town rope way transportation for particular area has also been introduced but still it has a great potentiality.

Uttar Pradesh State Roadways Transport Corporation (UPSRTC) provides deluxe bus service from Nainital to Delhi. As mentioned in Chapter 3, conducted tours are also available from Nainital for several destinations in the region. Conducted tour can be arranged from this town through KMOU or private bus owners. Ordinary and deluxe buses are available for this purpose. The popular conducted bus tours are as follows:

(a) Nainital-Bhimtal-Ghorakhal

(b) Nainital-Jim Corbett National Park

(c) Nainital-Delhi

(d) Nainital-Kausani

(e) Kumaun Darshan

Communication brings people and communities closer. At present mass communication are through various means, such as post, telegraph, telephone (including ISD booths), teleprinter, wireless, radio, newspaper, television, fax and movies. In the region, post, telegraph and telephone facility are adequate. Almost all the tourist centres in the region are connected by telephones. The district headquarters and other important places are served by wireless facilities. The station of the All India Radio is located in Almora and serves as a subsidiary centre to transmit news and other items. Further, there are cinema hall in sizeable centres, but video are becoming popular. The latter supplements the cinema houses and others means of entertainment.

Accommodation

There are two broad categories of tourist facilities:

(a) Basic necessity of the tourists and it may be also divided into two groups:

(i) Travel and transport
(ii) Boarding and lodging.

(b) Supporting facilities like literature, marketing, travel agents, tour operators, guides, sports, health and recreational facilities.

Tourism much depends on the basic facilities, while the growth depends on the supporting facilities. The transportation has been discussed earlier. But the most important factor is the accommodation facilities. It is also a major part of the expenditure. Recently, affluent people have become very particular about the quality of accommodation. Everybody expects comforts like their respective homes. There are a few good hotels as well. However, according to the Department of Tourism, Government of India, definition of hotel includes restaurants, beach resorts and other tourist complexes providing accommodation and/or catering and food facilities to tourists.

In the region there are tourist bungalows in several places which are run by the UP Tourist Department. There are other State government establishments as well, such as dak bungalows, guest houses, circuit houses and inspection bungalows. They belong to various State government departments and institutions. They are specially meant for official and State guests, but however prior reservations and personal contacts may be helpful in getting them.

TABLE 5.2 : Accommodation in Nainital and Almora Towns

Accommodation	Nainital		Almora	
	Centres	Beds	Centres	Beds
Hotels	42	2,232	13	395
Government Rest House	5	350	5	215
Dharmashalas	2	120	1	5
Religious Institutions	4	105	3	65
Others	42	2,300	NA	NA
TOTAL	95	5,107	22	680

Source : Survey by the authors.

Dharmashalas are important for the economically weaker tourists. During summer and winter seasons and also during religious fairs, this type of accommodation become popular. They provide supplementary facilities at a minimum cost. A few single tourists can be given lodging facilities here. However, the state of most of the dharmashalas is poor. There exists unhygienic conditions inside them and the environment is filthy as well. There is no proper arrangement of water and lavatory. Rooms are dark and humid. A traveller has to suffer due to mismanagement and other irregularities in these establishments. These dharamshalas exist in main towns of this region.

Establishments meant for providing accommodation in the region have to face the fluctuations in demand. This problem is specially acute in Nainital town during the summer and autumn seasons when a flood of tourists enters thereby causing a sudden jump in the hotel occupancy rate and also creating periodic shortage of accommodation during these seasons. The pressure of traffic is also increased and that results in a fall in their standards. During the off season, the establishments are not occupied to their full capacity which leads to the problem of maintenance and employment, thus fluctuation creates problems at both extremes. During the winter, when it is off period, visitors can be allured by providing enticements and concessions. Hence, the off season tourism is necessary in the region. The winter sports and games and other infrastructure should be developed if we want to promote tourism in the real sense. It is also necessary to satisfy the accommodation demands of tourists.

The management staff of the hotels is quite untrained. The opening of short term diploma courses in catering and hotel management will prove fruitful. Further, the paying guest system can also be profitable business for its residents, having sufficient potentiality for providing excess accommodation to the tourists.

Electricity

Electricity is an important infrastructural facility to support the improvement and now it has become the basic need of the people. Meeting the power requirements also provides a valuable support for improvement in agriculture and industries. No one can dream promotion of tourism without electricity. Having cold climate, besides scarcity of wood and coal, electricity only can give desired heat to the tourists coming from other areas to this comparatively cold climatic region. In the study region almost all tourist destinations are connected with the main electricity line and electrification net is also expanding rapidly all over the region.

Electricity in Nainital was locally introducted in the year 1922. Since then local residents and tourists of this destination are benefited by this facility. The tourists enjoy the attractions of twinkling light on the lake water while walking on the road at night. Local people and hoteliers are benefited from commercial point of view as well. Table 5.3 provides details about electric connections in Nainital and Almora towns.

TABLE 5.3 : Electric connections in Nainital and Almora towns

Type of connections	Numbers	
	Nainital	Almora
Domestic	6,043	6,212
Commercial	552	73
Industrial	13	349
Street lights	15	38
Water works	12	30
Miscellaneous	20	22
Total	6,655	6,724

Source : Electric Supply Divisions of Nagar Palika, Nainital and Hydel Office, Almora.

Almora has 6,724 electric connection in which 92.39 per cent are for domestic use while 5.12 per cent for industries, and 1.07 and 0.53 per cent are for commercial and street lights respectively.

Electricity was introduced to Ranikhet in 1962 which is controlled by the Hydel Department and Military Engineering Service (MES) while recently Kausani has been supplied electric connections.

Water Supply

Availability of drinking water is our fundamental need and most important factor of area development. In the study region there is plenty sources of natural water is obtainable through ponds, *nala* (springs), and perennial water channels. But people have been mostly using the facilities of taps and tanks. Water supply is either by gravity system (40 %) or by pumping (60 %). The required supply could not be met by these sources only. Due to this reason, Almora town suffers almost all the year round and this has also resulted in lesser tourist flow.

In 1950 Almora was introduced with pumping water supply and it was modernized in 1974-75. Drinking water supply is controlled and distributed by Uttar Pradesh Jal Nigam and Jal Sansthan. The Kosi river has been the major source of water while springs of Syahi Devi and Baldhoti have been working as alternative arrangements. Table 5.4 indicates the type of water connections in the two major urban centres of the region.

TABLE 5.4 : Water connections in Almora and Nainital towns

Type of connections	Number	
	Almora	Nainital
Domestic	2,662	2,571
Public stand-posts	120	140
Non-domestic	235	311
Fire hydrants	26	49
TOTAL	3,043	3,071

Source : Kumaun Jal Sansthan, Almora and Nainital, 1987.

The Military Engineering Services (MES) and the Cantonment Board are engaged in managing the water supply in Ranikhet where the water is collected from the springs. For civil population, about 90,480 gallons of water is supplied per day. Total water connections in this town are 547, whereas the total number of houses is 2,570. The tourists are supplied water through these limited outlets which are grossly insufficient.

Another tourist centre, Kausani, is trying to solve its water problem through the Rural Water Supply Scheme provided by the local authorities. The main sources of water are streams, falls and local water bodies. Now it is proposed that water will be pumped directly from the river Kosi and stored for distribution in the resort. Considering the present water supply, almost all the resorts are suffering from insufficient quantity which has adversely effected the tourism in the region.

Sewage and Drainage

Keeping in view the rapid growth of population in the several resorts, recently the Uttar Pradesh Jal Nigam has prepared the plan to improve the existing sewage and drainage disposal system. Before 1880, there was no proper system of drainage in this town. The landslip catastrophe of 1880 attracted the attention of the then authorities. In the beginning, the whole work was completed by the government, and later the Municipal Board was made responsible for its maintenance. The drainage system on Sher-ka-Danda, Ayarpatta, east and west Baranala and Lake Basin thus came into existence. The proper sewage system in Nainital was started in 1942 which now covers about 60 per cent population of this resort, while 40 per cent people are using their own private tanks. The total number of sewage connections are about 500.

No proper system of sewage and drainage exists in Almora. Night soil from individual houses and community latrine is carried out by the staff or Municipal Board and collected at a particular place outside the town. Kausani and Ranikhet, also face the problem of defective sewage and drainage systems. In these centres night soil is collected by patent carts and destroyed in incinerators.

Educational Facilities

Educational institutions have also played a vital role in promoting tourism in the area. Tourism has become popular by these institutions, such as schools, colleges, university, and technical and vocational institutions. Among them public school and technical training institutions are much popular. People coming to these institutions for themselves or their children also have an intention to visit different places of tourist curiosity. The tourist infrastructure is taken advantage of during the opening, closure and during exclusive functions in these institutions.

The recently opened Kumaun University is serving the region as well as other parts of the country through a number of government, semi-government and private colleges. In the region, this university has two campuses, one at Nainital and other in Almora. Table 5.5 displays the educational centres in the three most important resorts of the region.

TABLE 5.5 : Educational Institutions

Place	Schools		Colleges		University	Technical Institute
	Pri.	Jr. High	Inter	Degree		
Nainital	24	5	5	–	1	2
Almora	18	4	6	1	1	3
Ranikhet	8	3	3	1	–	1
TOTAL	50	12	14	2	2	6

Source : Basic Education office and District Inspector of School Offices at above places.

Medical Facilities

The resorts of the regions have started their real development during the British period which included the opening up of medical and health facilities. Due to the better quality of environment, T.B. sanatoriums and clinics were established in Bhowali and Almora, while Bageshwar and Bhimtal became primary health centre. Further, there is Govind Ballabh Pant Hospital, Badri Dutt Pande Hospital and Sitapur Eye Hospital in Nainital. Similarly, Almora has several hospitals, such as Civil Hospital, Civil Hospital for Women, Sitapur Eye Hospital, Leprosy Hospital and Ayurvedic Hospital. Further, Ranikhet also has three hospitals. The T.B.

sanatorium in Bhowali is well known. Other tourists resorts also have similar facilities which are not only used by the population of the region but also from other parts of the country.

Tourists Guides and Operators

Tourists guides and operators have a role to play in promoting tourism. In Nainital, guides can be arranged by advance notice and request through Tourist Bureau, Himalayan Tourist Corporation and Kumaun Travels. Similarly, various agencies, including Tourist Bureau can provide guides in Almora. From Nainital, the places like Ranikhet, Kausani, Baijnath and Bhimtal are generally included in conducted tours with guides. In several places, the hotels provide guides for a group of tourists. The Jim Corbett National Park also provides guides for watching wild life.

At present, all conducted tour agencies have been operating from Nainital. They generally have luxury buses. Tourists much depends on such facilities. Bus transport is very important in the area as it is least served by railways. Conducted tour is very important in this region as it provides transportation, and boarding and lodging facilities without hassles.

Other Facilities

In Nainital region lakes provides vast opportunity for recreation both for domestic and foreign tourists. Country made boats are being used for boating. Clubs, cinemas, picnic spots, petrol pumps and catering facilities are providing one of the best opportunities in the country. However, there is a scope for further improvement. The Boathouse club and Nainital club are the famous in the region. Sport stadium is situated at Nainital, while a big golf course is in Ranikhet.

A good amount of literature, both in Hindi and English are available in the region and other towns as well, but only a few of them are able to give detailed knowledge about tourism in the region. Most of the books are exclusively dealing with the religious glory and shrines but cannot provide with basic information. In English, a large number of books are written about India in which the cities of the region have been described. Much popular and useful books about the region are the *Himalayan Gazetteer* written by Atkinson and *Kumaun ka Itihas* by Shri Badri Dutt Pande. These books contain information on tourist interest as well.

Shopping forms an integral part of tourism. In the region foreign tourists normally spend only a little amount out of their expenditure on shopping while domestic tourist of every income group buy some items which is specific of the region, such as woollen clothes and souvenirs.

On the whole, civic amenities and public utility based services at tourist centres are sufficient. Almost all the resorts have limited facilities to extent to the tourists, while Nainital has too much to offer to the tourists as well as to the local residents. The existing facilities are to be improved further in order to meet the requirements of the local and tourist population. The facilities are particularly lacking at the intermediate points between the resorts. The concerned authorities should encourage the local inhabitants to provide fresh milk of coffee and refreshments. There should be sufficient toilet facilities as well.

REFERENCES

Atkinson, E.T. (1973) *The Himalayan Gazetteer*, Cosmos Publication, New Delhi (reprint).

Atkinson, E.T. (1974) *Kumaun Hills*, Cosmos Publication, New Delhi (reprint).

Nevilli, H.R. (1904), *District Gazetteer: Nainital*, Vol. I, XXXIV and XXXV.

Joshi, S.C. *et al.* (1983), *Kumaun Himalaya-Geographical Perspective on Resource Development*, Gyanodaya Prakashan, Nainital.

Pande, B.D. (1936), *Kumaun ka Itihas*, Almora Shakti Press, Almora

Pandey, T. (1962), *Kumaun ka Lok Sahitya*, Almora Book Depot, Almora.

Chapter 6

TOURIST RESPONSE AND PREFERENCES

After having an appraisal of assorted aspects of tourists infrastructure of the region, it is crucial to know how do the tourists react to such facilities. What are there responses and preferences? Are the responses specific to the income level of certain community? What are the requisites of different population groups? These questions are most pertaining in order to have a strategy for (a) selection of resort for tourism, and (b) development of a tourist resort. In order to do so, it was obligatory to collect information regarding the origin, purpose, class, age group, income pattern, educational level, occupation, accommodation and mode of transportation availed, and the like. From the foreign tourists, it was important to know the amount of foreign exchange spent in the region.

Coming in contact with a very limited number of person, a tourist may gather an impression about a resort. He will have sweet or sour memories about the place depending upon the type of persons he has to come across. Nainital region has also its share of every kind of people, ranging from extreme hospitable and well behaved to antisocials. Unfortunately, a tourist has to come across the whole variety. For the sake of convenience, the complete year has been divided into three seasons : viz. (a) summers, from mid March to mid June, (b) autumn, from mid September to mid November, and (c) others, the remaining period. The latter comprises of rainy season from mid June to mid September, and winter season from mid November to mid March. The information collected through interviews of about 500 tourists are based on these seasons.

Domestic and International Tourists

In order to make an assessment for the development of tourism, on one hand, it is necessary to make distinction between the domestic and international tourists, though both may be stranger to the place; while on the other, to understand their different socio-economic background. Table 6.1 indicates the number of tourists belonging to various religious groups who have visited the area during 1988. From this table it is evident that the number of Hindu visitors exceeds others mainly due to the existence of historical places of Hindu religion. This shows that apart from the other factors the religious importance of a place attracts people of that faith in good numbers (Fig 6.1).

TABLE 6.1 : Religion and tourism

Religion	No. of tourists	Percentage
Hindus	370	74
Muslims	50	10
Sikhs	35	7
Christians	15	3
Others	30	6

Source : Fieldwork by the authors.

Purpose of Visit

It is not easy to classify the tourists according to the purpose of visit. They generally move in a group or family, and all the members of the group may not have the single purpose for the visits. Some of them have only intention of accompanying their friends or relatives. However, common interest can always be found out. First of all the pleasure is the most significant reason followed by study or educational tour. Business has been another important reason for travelling, preferably combined with official tour. However, regarding the foreign tourists, business and other similar

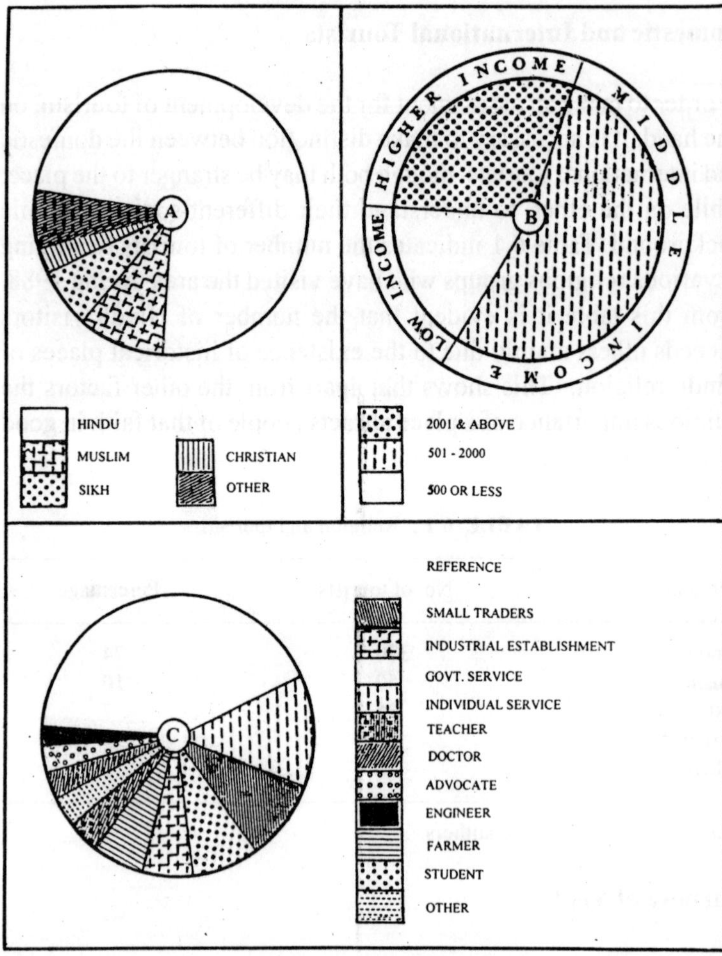

FIG. 6.1 : Categories of Tourists According to Religion Income and Occupation

tasks may not be of much significance. Their purpose of visiting is primarily to enjoy the calm and quiet atmosphere. They get fed up with the mechanical and organised way of life and therefore they want new tranquillity and deviations. Thus they select hilly region like Nainital. Moreover, the domestic tourist visit this region to study the archaeological and historical monuments (Table 6.2).

TABLE 6.2 : Occupation of tourists

Occupation	Number	Percentage
Small traders	52	10.04
Industrial establishments	10	6.00
Government service	212	42.35
Private sector	65	13.00
Teacher	19	3.75
Doctor	15	3.00
Advocate	15	3.00
Engineer	10	2.00
Farmer	30	6.00
Student	35	7.00
Others	17	3.40
TOTAL	500	100.00

Source : Fieldwork by the authors.

Following the religious and occupational composition of the tourists, the income pattern is important to work out a strategy for the development of tourism. Table 6.3 shows the economic composition of the tourists. It indicates that the majority are from the middle income group (Fig. 6.1B).

TABLE 6.3 : Tourism and income levels

Income level	Income per month (Rs.)	No. of Tourists	%
High	More than 2,000	144	28.8
Middle	501-2,000	266	53.6
Low	Less than 500	88	17.6
TOTAL		500	100.00

Source : Fieldwork by the authors

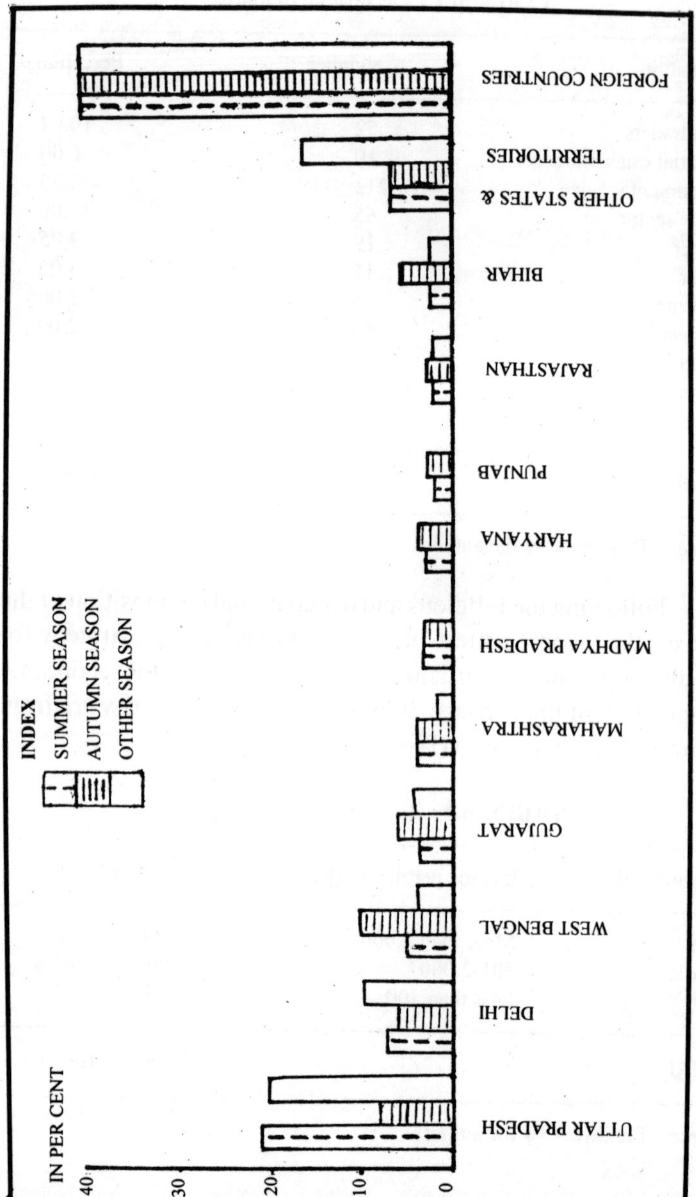

FIG. 6.2 : Origin of Tourists : National and International

Regional Pattern

Table 6.4 reveals that the region has received a considerable number of domestic tourists from Uttar Pradesh, Delhi and West Bengal : 21.00, 7.33 and 5.00 per cent respectively during the summer season. On the other hand, in autumn, tourists from West Bengal followed by Uttar Pradesh and Delhi were the most. The foreign tourist has almost constant figure of nearly 40 per cent during all the three seasons (Fig. 6.2).

TABLE 6.4 : Domestic and international tourists

State of origin	Summer Season		Autumn Season		Other Season	
	No.	%	No.	%	No.	%
Uttar Pradesh	63	21.00	13	8.67	10	20.00
Delhi	22	7.33	10	6.67	5	10.00
West Bengal	15	5.00	16	10.66	2	4.00
Gujarat	11	3.67	9	6.00	2	4.00
Maharashtra	12	4.00	6	4.00	1	2.00
Madhya Pradesh	9	3.00	5	3.33	—	—
Haryana	8	2.67	5	3.33	—	—
Punjab	6	2.00	4	2.67	—	—
Rajasthan	7	2.33	4	2.67	1	2.00
Bihar	7	2.33	8	5.33	1	2.00
Other states/ UTs	20	6.67	10	6.67	8	16.00
Abroad	120	40.00	60	40.00	20	40.00
TOTAL	300	100.00	150	100.00	50	100.00

Source : Fieldwork by the authors.

Purpose of Visit

It is not easy to classify the tourists according to the purposes of visit. They generally move in a group or family, and all the members of the group may not have the single purpose for the visits. Some of them have only intention of accompanying their friends or relatives. However, common interest can always be found out. First of all the pleasure is the most significant reason followed by study or educational tour. Business has been another important reason for travelling, preferably combined with official tour. However, regarding the foreign tourists, business and other similar tasks may not be of much significance. Their purpose of visits is primarily to enjoy the calm and quiet atmosphere. They get fed up with the technical and scientific way of life and therefore they want new tranquillity and deviations. Thus they select hilly region like Nainital. Moreover, the domestic tourist visit this region to study the archaeological and historical monuments, such as of Baijnath, Jageshwar, Almora, and Katarmal. Most of them like to have a glance of snow covered mountain peaks and ridges seen from Kausani and Ranikhet and to get fruitful and flourishing views of Chaubattia, Ramgarh, Mukteshwar and Jalna. They also like to enjoy the resort towns of Nainital and Bhimtal as well. Jim Corbett National Park falls in different category.

As indicated earlier, most of the visitors interviewed had more than a single purpose for visiting the region. This region in general and Nainital in particular is famous for pleasure and honeymoon which is mostly in the summers. The pilgrims would like to visit the religious places mostly in autumn. The businessmen and official do not have any specific time, but they would prefer to visit in summers. This is also the time of visits of friends, conferences and schools. The purpose of visits can be observed from the Table 6.5.

TABLE 6.5 : Tourists and purpose of visits

Purpose	SUMMER		AUTUMN		OTHER	
	No.	%	No.	%	No.	%
Pleasure/honeymoon	142	47.21	68	45.70	20	39.80
Business	23	7.59	9	5.68	5	9.32
Pilgrimage	35	11.69	46	30.64	12	23.91

Contd.

Table 6.5 (*Contd.*)

Purpose	SUMMER		AUTUMN		OTHER	
	No.	%	No.	%	No.	%
Study	45	15.15	9	9.05	2	5.48
Official	19	6.28	8	5.12	5	10.09
Friends/ relatives	18	6.00	5	3.27	3	6.25
Other	18	6.08	5	3.54	3	5.15

Source : Fieldwork by the authors.

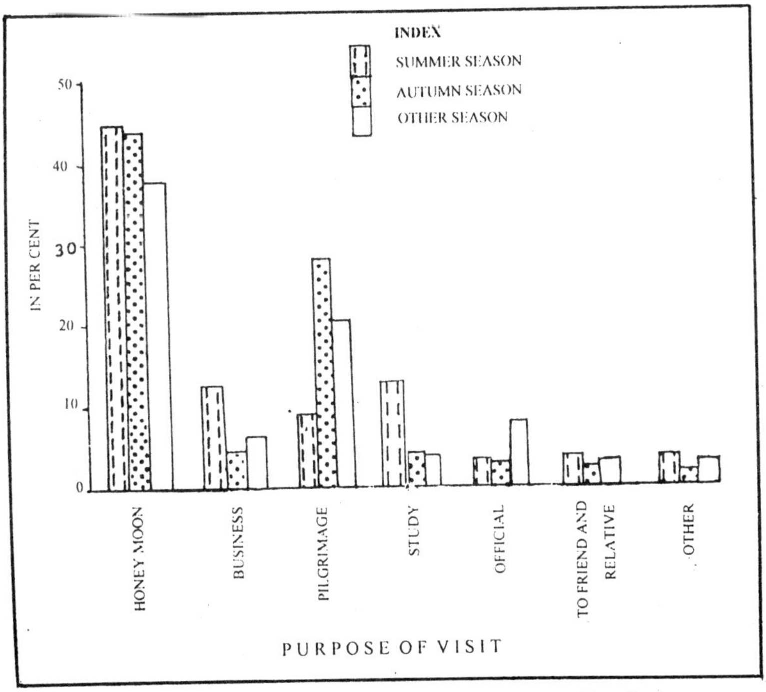

FIG. 6.3 : Aspects of Tourism : Tourists and their Visiting Purpose

Age-Sex Structure

The composition of population is important consideration for the success of the development of tourism. The children require milk

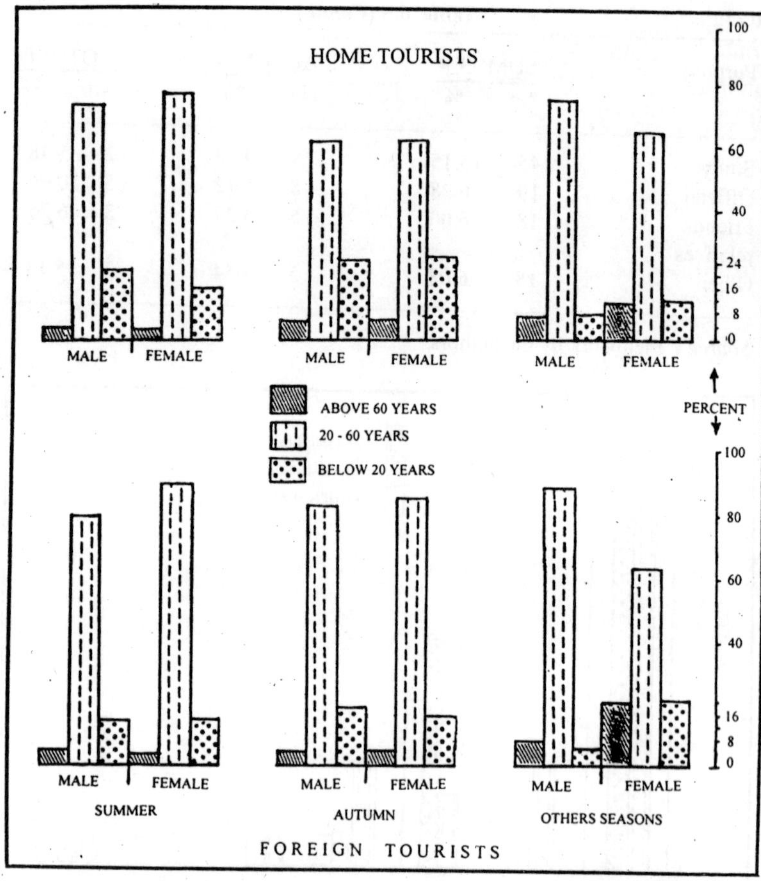

FIG. 6.4 : Distribition of Tourists according to their age and sex structure

supply, parks, playgrounds and amusement centres, while adults are very much fond of recreational facilities meant for them, such as cinemas, clubs and bars. The senior citizens would like to have quiet places like riverside, temples or scenic spot. Table 6.6 shows the distributions of tourists according to age-sex structure. The percentage of male and female tourists in the age group of below 20 years was 21.30 and 15.27 per cent respectively, and was 6.48 males and 4.17 per cent females in the age group of above 60 years. Further, in the age group of 20 to 60 years it constitutes highest percentage of males and females i.e. 72.22 and 60.56 per cent respectively during the summer season. The percentage of foreign tourists was also high in the same season within the age group of 20-60 years (84.72% males and 87.50% females respectively). During the autumn season, the percentage of domestic and foreign tourists in the same age group was high as well. The percentage of domestic tourists in the age group of above 60 years comparatively increases during autumn due to so-called Bengali season. Percentage of foreign tourists during the autumn and other season (winter and spring) have an increase in each age group because of favourable climatic conditions. In the other months the percentage of domestic tourists in the age group of 20-60 years was 85.72 per cent males and 77.78 per cent females; and the percentage of foreign tourists 85.72 for males and 66.66 for females (Table 6.6). In the age group of above 60 years, it was 4.67 per cent males and 11.11 per cent females respectively. The region received 9.52 per cent males and 11.11 per cent females of the domestic tourists and 7.14 and 16.67 percent males and females of the foreign tourists during the same season in the age group of below 20 years (Fig. 6.4).

TABLE 6.6 : Tourists according to age-groups

Season	Below 20		20-60		Above 60		Total	
	No.	%	No.	%	No.	%	No.	%
			SUMMER					
Domestic								
Male	23	21.30	78	72.22	7	6.48	108	100
Female	11	15.27	58	80.56	3	4.17	72	100
Foreign								
Male	8	11.11	61	84.72	3	4.17	72	100
Female	5	10.42	42	87.50	1	2.08	48	100
			AUTUMN					
Domestic								
Male	16	25.39	42	66.67	5	7.94	63	100
Female	7	25.93	18	66.67	2	7.60	27	100

(*Contd.*)

Table 6.6 (*Contd.*)

Season	Below 20 No.	%	20-60 No.	%	Above 60 No.	%	Total No.	%
			AUTUMN					
Foreign								
Male	6	14.29	35	80.93	2	4.26	42	100
Female	2	11.11	15	83.33	1	5.56	18	100
			OTHER					
Domestic								
Male	2	9.52	18	85.72	1	4.76	21	100
Female	1	11.11	7	77.78	1	11.11	9	100
Foreign								
Male	1	7.14	12	85.72	1	7.14	14	100
Female	1	16.67	4	66.66	1	16.67	6	100

Source : Fieldwork by the Authors.

Mode of Travel

The several options for reaching this region have been discussed earlier. People do prefer to travel in a package tour programme by bus from major cities like Delhi, Lucknow and Calcutta. Generally long distance passengers choose this option. Use of Private vehicles or cars are common for a visiting family from a higher income group. There is no facility for air transport in the region. The nearest airport is situated in Pantnagar which is connected by bus service with Nainitial.

It is obvious from the Table 6.7 that most of the tourists travel by buses throughout the year. The other common option is the rental car. During summer, autumn and other seasons, about 13, 18.67 and 26 per cent people have used this mode respectively. The third common mode is personal cars, which is mostly in summer season (Fig. 6.5).

TABLE 6.7 : Mode of travel of the tourists

Mode of Travel	Summer		Autumn		Other	
Motor Bus	204	68.00	92	61.33	27	54.00
Rental Car	39	13.00	28	18.67	13	26.00
Private Car	33	11.00	18	12.00	6	12.00
Others	24	8.00	12	8.00	4	8.00
TOTAL	300	100.00	150	100.00	50	100.00

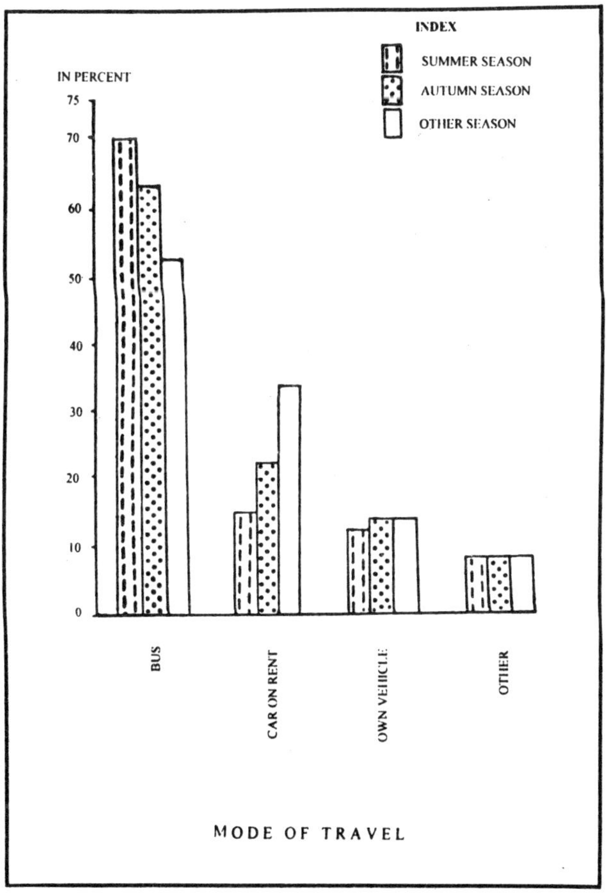

FIG. 6.5 : Mode of Travel

It has been noticed that the mode of travel is very vital for planning the programmes in general and time frame in particular. Travelling by bus has increased due to the expansion of travel organizations. People from the neighbouring districts have no choice but to travel by buses. Against this, the mode of travel partially by rail is not preferred much. Only long distance passengers choose this to reach either the railhead or to a major city to avail bus service. Students and pilgrims also some time prefer to come by this mode. They make reservations well in advance.

Preference for Accommodation

The resorts of the study region faces the accommodation problems during the peak tourist season. It is observed that a large number of tourists prefer accommodation in comparatively cheap hotels and government accommodation facilities. This is followed by *dharamshala* and houses of friends and relatives. Table 6.8 indicates the type of accommodation availed in the region during different seasons. This pattern may not exactly indicate the preferences of the tourists which is likely to be governed by certain compulsions, such as cost, availability and communication.

TABLE 6.8 : Type of accommodation availed

Type of accommodation	Summer		Autumn		Other	
	No.	%	No.	%	No.	%
Hotel	201	67.00	57	38.00	20	40.00
Dharamshala	21	7.00	34	22.66	7	14.00
Government Rest House	50	20.00	40	26.66	10	20.00
Friends/ Relatives	15	5.00	12	8.00	13	26.00
Rental houses	3	1.00	7	4.60	—	—
TOTAL	300	100.00	150	100.00	50	100.00

Source : Field survey by the authors.

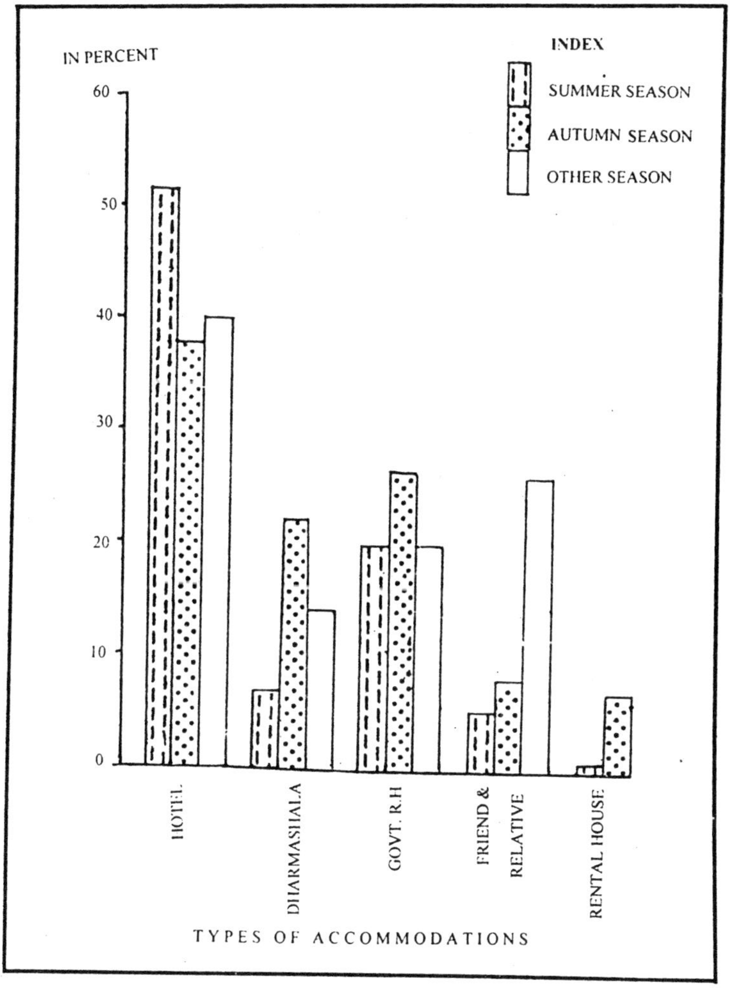

FIG. 6.6 : Types of Accommodations in the Region

Income and Expenditure

The impact of tourism on employment and income is closely interrelated as they are associated with the expenditure which a tourist makes during his stay. In this region it has been noticed with the help of questionnaire that the majority of the domestic tourists belong to the middle and lower middle income groups. However, the number of tourists from the higher income group is increasing gradually. In case of foreign tourists they belong to the middle and higher income groups. A large number of tourists from abroad prefer to visit India because it is cheap in comparison than to countries. Even one can find foreign students visiting this region.

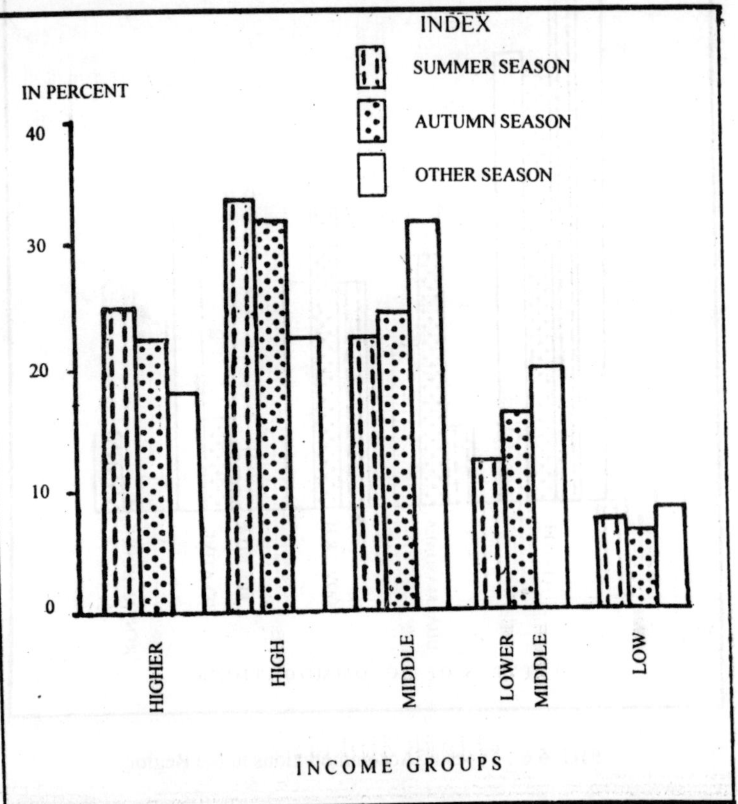

FIG. 6.7 : Tourist Visits during Different Seasons (Based on income group)

Table 6.9 is based on the questionnaire. It is obvious from this table that the high and very high income groups of tourists constitutes about 34 and 25 per cent respectively during the summer season; while 22, 12 and 7 per cent belong to the middle, lower middle and poor income groups in the same season. The tourists of middle and lower middle income groups increase during the autumn season to 24 and 16 per cent respectively. In other seasons of the year, it increase gradually to about 32 and 20 per cent respectively.

TABLE 6.9 : Income groups of the tourists

Income group	SUMMER		AUTUMN		OTHER	
	No.	%	No.	%	No.	%
Very High	75	25	33	22	9	18
High	102	34	48	32	11	22
Middle	66	22	36	24	16	32
Lower middle	36	12	24	16	10	20
Low	21	7	9	6	4	8
TOTAL	300	100	150	100	50	100

Source : Fieldwork by the authors.

The expenditure of a tourist depends positively on the duration of the stay in the region. It has been observed that high income group tourists stayed more and spend more as well than the relatively low income group visitors. They purchase local handicrafts and other expensive items, and add a significant amount to the economy of the region. Whereas the lower middle and low income group tourists go for small articles such as toys, bangles, ordinary ornaments and the like. They are generally pilgrims and hence have a different attitude towards their visits to the region.

Motivational Aspects

Most of the tourists visiting the Nainital region are mainly inspired by their self decision. Nevertheless, magazines, travel and guide books, newspapers, journals, radio and television etc have inspired such tourists to visit the region. Previous experiences are also important in this regard. During this study it was found that about 25 per cent of interviewed domestic tourists have visited the region earlier, while only 2 per cent of the foreign tourists were making repeat visits. The latter were mostly interested in the Jim Corbett National Park.

Among the tourist resorts of the region, a considerable number of tourists gave preference to Nainital and subsequently to the Jim Corbett National Park, Bhimtal, Ranikhet and then Almora. However, the case of the foreign tourists was different. They prefer Almora and Jim Corbett National Park and thereafter Baijnath, Ranikhet and finally Nainital. The similar trend was also observed while enquiring about the itinerary of the tourists. About 40 per cent of the domestic tourists preferred to spent much of their time in Nainital and around. This also due to the lack of infrastructure facilities in other resorts. On the other hand, the foreign tourists would like to stay more in Almora and the Jim Corbett National Park.

Reactions of Tou.. ists

It has been gathered through the questionnaire and interviews that a considerable number of domestic tourists are strongly dissatisfied about the behaviours of the guides, agents and shopkeepers who always try to charge more for their services or products. Many foreign tourists found Nainital as a expensive city and is much commercialized. Though Nainital is a mini cosmopolitan city, a number of domestic tourists were extra critical and disappointed than the foreign tourists. A large number of tourists complain about the quality of food which was average. The services were poor and unhygienic. Further, the quality of water and limited supply and unreasonable charges for accommodation are some of the issues which the tourists strongly feel. Another group of tourists were more concerned about the wider issues, like pollution of the lake and the decay of the historical monuments.

The foreign tourists consider the accommodation facilities as excellent or very good. The contradiction in the opinion of the quality of accommodation between the domestic and foreign tourists is due to their capacity to hire such places. However, both types of tourists have mentioned about unsuitable and uncomfortable transport services. The conditions of the roads in the remote areas is not good. Non-availability of buses and other means of transport were also the causes of disappointments. The bus services of the Kumaun Mandal Vikas Nigam were appreciated. The behaviours of the local people was nevertheless appreciated by both types of visitors. Only a few of the domestic tourists have contacted the government tourists information centres while almost all foreign tourists have obtained desired information from such offices located in various places.

Although the tourist industry is considered as the backbone of the economy of the region, yet the tourist centres have comparatively failed to attract much visitors from far away areas due to lack of transport, accommodation, congestion and poor professional management. The other suggestions by the tourists mainly relate to guides and agents, better medical facilities at various halts, availability of guide maps, toilet facilities and the most important accommodation. A considerable number of tourists would like to have hotels at different places like Mukteshwar, Ramgarh, Jageshwar etc. so that the tourists could be diverted to these centres.

If the above reactions are some indications for improvements, the tourist departments at the centre and of the State Government of Uttar Pradesh as well as the local authorities will have to take appropriate steps soon. Individual and integrated resort development have to be considered. More determined initiatives are required in this direction as such steps will surely improve the local economy of the region.

REFERENCES

Bradnock, Robert (1997), *India Handbook*, Footprint Hand books, Bath (U.K.), pp. 191-241.

Kaur, J. (1980), Re-evaluating Nainital tourism capacity for diffusion : Planned tourism activity in the Kumaun Lake Basins, in Singh, T.V (ed), *Studies in Himalayan Ecology and Development Strategies*, The English Book Store, New Delhi.

Kayastha, S.L. (1997), Tourism and environment in the Himalayan region in P. Nag, V.K. Kumra & J. Singh (eds), *Geography and Environment : Regional Issues*, Concept Publishing Company, New Delhi, pp. 31-45.

Kayastha, S.L and Rai, H.C. (1983), Nainital : A case Study in Tourism, *Hill Geographer*, Vol. 2, No. 2.

NATMO (1984), *Tourist Atlas of India*, National Atlas & Thematic Mapping Organisation, Calcutta.

Chapter 7

ADVENTURE TOURISM : TREKKING

There is no site as much for trekking in the region, but it has proved to be a base for trekking to the lesser Himalayan region lying in the north. Several of the resorts do cater to the needs of the trekkers as well. Hence, a special emphasis has been given to assess the facilities for trekking in the region. It is a distinct type of tourism which has lately become popular with the hs. Trekkers are different from the tourists who visit Nainital or Ranikhet or Jim Corbett National Park. Their life is full of adventure. They use their physical and mental courage, patience, and spirit to enjoy the nature in wilderness.

Himalaya has attracted adventurers, wanderers, scientists, students, teachers, researchers for a long time. In most cases, it is a lifelong dedication. One of the best way to know Himalaya is obviously trekking. In spite of the great popularity, there is not much information available to the intending tourist which could be used for guidance. Trekking in the region implies going to the hills which are situated away from the conventional tourists resorts such as Nainital, Almora and Ranikhet.

There has been concern all over about the Himalayan environment. The trekkers are expected to maintain, conserve and protect the environment as well so that it can be cherished in its original form. At the lower elevations, there are rich forests, beautiful natural scenery and a variety of flowers, rivers, trees, temples and people. At the higher elevations, one comes across rocks, streams snow and glaciers. The natural beauty is composed of high peaks touching the sky, a variety of vegetation, rugged rocks, steep slopes and the like. One may tend to become a poet to describe this beauty. The first hand information has its own distinction.

There are various routes, places and treks for every type of trekker. On certain routes and treks, local porters and mules are available to accompany the trekkers. Further, there are rest houses, dak bungalows, schools, private houses or even caves for the night stay. However, in the region, trekking is not an organized activity excepting that there is a Officer-on-Special-Duty, Sports Department in Almora and a few unknown clubs. An institute for trekking in the region would be most appropriate for supporting such an activity.

PLANNING A TREKKING PROGRAMME

A special care has to be taken for planning a trekking programme as it is different from other type of tourism where every requirement can be bought by money. Trekking needs patience, courage, spirit, physical fitness and will power besides money. A trekker has to be acquainted and prepared for hardship of any sort. He must collect relevant information and take suggestions from other trekking organizations and individuals. However, some of issues have been discussed here.

Geographical Background

Trekking is generally done on mountainous regions. The routes are rough, tough and difficult for walking. Besides the information on routes, an idea of the climatic conditions is necessary particularly when the trekkers are from the plains where the conditions are just the opposite. A trekker is advised to carry warm clothes or wind proof jackets. It is difficult to walk and breathe while going up the mountains beyond the tree zone. Even in the month of June, there is chilled cold at the higher elevations. A trekker may not feel cold while walking but while taking rest, the sweat dries up and he starts feeling cold.

Every trekking route has its different geographical phenomenon in the region. A few resorts are common for trekking while many places are not preferred by the trekkers. Kumaun Himalaya which is just beyond the Nainital region offers incomparable opportunities for the trekkers. Hence, a large number of trekkers visit every year. The northeastern part is the secluded region, rugged, extreme mountainous and lies on the bank of Gori Ganga which makes the international boundary. Nevertheless, this part of the region is popular with the trekkers because of its uniqueness and average elevation over 4,000 m.

PHYSICAL AND MENTAL FITNESS

In order to enjoy trekking during the holidays, one should be physically and mentally fit, apart from many other qualities. He should be daily jogging and should be practising physical and mental exercises. A trekker needs a lot of patience for adjustment with his fellow trekker, team leader or organizers in order to face difficult situations. People tend to become irritated due to non acclimatization and other discomforts. Such a participant should be free from acute diseases. Necessary precautions may also be taken against malaria. Some may not have comfortable sleeps due to high altitude. Smoking should preferably be prohibited.

Clothing and Equipments

Equipments and clothing are extremely essential part of the preparations. A check list must be prepared by the trekker himself or by the group leader. Although both these items are not very special yet some items are not used in our daily life. Both the types of items should be very light so that they can be carried easily, and can be protected from rain, snow and cold and strong winds. Carrying load itself is a difficult task. The temperature changes very quickly from hot day to cold and chilly nights in high elevations. Strong winds are common. The selection of clothing and equipments hence is very important for a trekking initiative.

Some details are as follows :

Clothing

Loose clothes are comfortable but differs from person to person. Due to cold, it is near impossible to have a bath, so a few pairs of extra undergarments are needed but in some places bath is possible even then these pair of clothes are required. A trekker generally needs a pair of old trousers, shorts, skirts, shirts and jumper etc. Jeans are best companion due to the strength of the cloth and possibility of using them without washing or ironing for a long time. But they should not be very light. Most of the trekkers prefer trousers with additional pockets. Shorts are also used for walking for easy movement. The ladies and girls can wear skirts if they do not like trousers or jeans. Woollen shirts and jumpers are imperative besides the cotton ones. For morning, evening and cold nights, a woollen pullover is essential, but it should be light and of good quality. A wind proof jacket is always good to protect from cold winds and rains. They are light to carry and comfortable to use. A pair of woollen or leather gloves will be useful for the hands to protect from snow and chilly winds. The trekkers are advised to take woollen socks and stockings which should be washed and changed frequently as dirty socks are the cause of blisters and bad smell. Powder may be carried as well. It is very important that the feet are trouble free during trekking. Two pairs of old used shoes may be carried.

Equipments

In addition to clothing, sun glasses or goggles are needed in the higher elevations where there is snow and ice. A strong glare can affect the eyes so badly that onecan not feel normal for a couple of days. A woollen hat or cap is also needed for the protection of face and neck. Trekkers do get sun burnt. A balaclaya can be a good substitute which will protect ears and neck as well. A very

A. Enchanting Himalaya from Kausani

B. Human settlement in Rural Kumaun

PLATE – XI

light rain coat is also needed for rain and snow. A trekker must have a good quality light rucksack for comfortable carrying of the belongings. A strong stick is also helpful in many ways.

Camp equipments are generally provided by the officer-in-charge at Almora or by the organisers which includes tents. If required, mattresses, sleeping bags with inner wind proof jackets, first aid kits, food and drinks and kitchen utensils can also be obtained. Sleeping bags may be optional as some of the regular trekkers would like to use their own. Table 7.1 provides a list of items required for planning a trekking programme.

TABLE 7.1 : Checklist for trekkers

A. CLOTHES AND EQUIPMENTS

1. Rucksack
2. Sleeping bag with inner wind proof lining
3. Shoes or boots with extra laces
4. Two pairs of socks
5. Underwear-4
6. Trousers-2
7. Shorts-1
8. Woollen Pullover-1
9. Shirt/T-shirts-4
10. Wind proof jacket
11. Gloves
12. Hat
13. Rain coat
14. Walking stick

B. WASHING KIT

1. Towels-2
2. Tooth paste and brush
3. Soap
4. Comb
5. Toilet paper
6. Powder and cream
7. Mirror
8. Shaving and personal requirements for gents and ladies

Contd.

Table 7.1 (*Contd.*)

C. GENERAL
1. Lighter, torch and candles
2. Water bottle and knife
3. Note book and pencil/pen
4. Sewing kit and nail cutter
5. Binocular and camera (if permitted)
6. Biscuits (1 packet per day) and Toffee (5 per day)

D. MEDICAL
1. Small first aid box
2. Usual medicines for headache, fever, stomach, diarrhoea, cold, constipation, throat lozenges, water purification tablets, eye drops, lotions, vitamin cancan tablets (2 daily), zinc cream, face cream, plaster, bandages, cotton etc.

E. FOOD MATERIALS
1. Rice, flour, dal, spices, sugar
2. Tea, coffee, biscuits, namkeen
3. Toffees, bournvita, milk
4. Dry fruits, fruits, vegetables
5. Butter, paneer, chips etc.

F. FOOD PACKETS
1. Fried grams
2. Drinks
3. Glucose
4. Tinned fish or meat
5. Jam tinned milk

All these articles from the above list, except the first-aid box, should be kept in the rucksack so that it is not left behind. Evidently, these articles have to be very light. Some of the above materials can be arranged on rent or from the officer-in -charge in Almora. The companies from where the equipments are available on hire are : Hill Top Tours and Travels, Nainital, Alka Excursions, Anamika Excursions, Trishul Travels, The Mall Nainital; and Shikhar Hotel, Almora. Further, there are firms in Delhi which supply some of the important items specifically required for trekking. They are as follows :

A. The Sylvan Countryside around Bageshwar (Almora)

B. The Flat's – Nainital favourite meeting place

PLATE – XII

1. M/s Supreme Mountaineering Equipment Industries (P) Ltd.
   49, Fazal Building, Ajmeri Gate, Delhi-110006.
2. M/s West Coast Manufacturers and Traders,
   261, Okhla Industrial Estate, New Delhi-110020.
3. Ibex Equipment,
   77, Friends Colony, New Delhi-110065.

In addition to above, various other firms located in Calcutta, Chennai, Mumbai and Kanpur and other cities have firms dealing with such equipments.

Maps and Related Information

Maps and other relevant information are available with the Tourist Officer at Almora, Nainital, Ranikhet; officer-on-special Duty (Sports Department), Almora; and Kumaun Vikas Mandal offices. In addition, various news agencies and clubs provide maps and books about trekking. But for a few places no detailed maps can be procured in the region as some of the maps are restricted due to security reasons. Government does allow publication of the maps with some limitations. However, trekking map of the region has been included which shows routes and places with approximate heights but without contours. Such sketch maps have been prepared particularly for trekking purposes. Regarding the description of various routes, all possible information has been provided. The heights and distances are approximate.

Trekking Season

The season and timing may differ from destination to destination in the same region. This type of adventure tourism can be of two types :

(a) Glacier trekking, and
(b) Non-glacier trekking.

Glacier Trekking

The best season for glacier trekking in from June to mid October, excluding the rains as the routes become very dangerous basically due to landslides. If the trekker wants to enjoy snow, end of May to mid June is the best period. Another period, September to mid October is also good due to rich natural vegetation. Further, there are several trekking places which do not have glacier area. Low elevation hills are important ones particularly from where snow peaks are clearly visible. However, there are several health resorts which are interesting for the trekkers all the year round.

Non-glacier trekking

The trek should be initiated in the morning hours carrying lunch packet along with them. The weather is clear during the morning. By noon fog and clouds are seen in the higher altitudes. Camping, programming, lecturing about environment, reading and gathering about local information should be done in the evenings. Some of the adventurous ones go for trekking even in the months of December and January to the glacier regions which is most dangerous. Nainital, Almora, Ranikhet and other local service centres are open all the days even from morning to late evening for shopping. The local people know only Hindi, hence it is advantageous to know this language. However, a few persons who can understand English can be found.

Preparations

There are different ways for reaching this region for trekking initiatives. A foreign trekker will prefer to come in the region by bus from Delhi while the domestic trekkers may arrive Haldwani or Kathgodam by train or bus. From these two places buses are frequently available to all the required destinations. Individual trekker can make arrangements in the region itself, provided they have rucksack or they contact the local authorities, i.e. Kumaun

Vikas Mandal, Nainital, Bageshwar and the Tourist Office at Nainital, Almora and Ranikhet. Here facilities are available for trekking to the Pindari Glacier. Kumaun Vikas Mandal has constructed the rest houses for tourists and trekkers and about Rupees eight hundred is charged per head for providing all the facilities, except personal porter. But other routes do not have such facilities and the trekkers have to make their own arrangements as per their programmes. The group leader of the trekking team are advised to contact, one or two months in advance, with the local authorities, i.e. Deputy Collector, District Education Officer or Officer on Special Duty in Almora for making arrangements such as reservation for lodging and boarding, porters, equipments etc. The Officer on Special Duty in Almora generally organizes such trekking programmes for ten days from May to October. The domestic trekkers (students, teachers, players, officials and youth groups) are advised to contact this officer for extending facilities. No payment is required for this purpose. The Government of Uttar Padesh provides free of charge the facilities such as guides, equipments, tents, lodging and even initial training for the beginners. Many other training programmes are also provided like crossing the river, rock climbing etc.

Popular Trekking Routes and Places

In order to find out the preferences of the trekkers, a survey was conducted out by the authors in 1989 and 1990. There are innu-merable treks through the region, small and wide cross-regional movements at lower altitudes is possible for a determined trekker. However, the region offers more varied and richer experience. The landscape changes from lush to comparatively less trodden, which however represent a picture of peace, tranquillity, solitude and wilderness. One can get totally absorbed in the vast stretches of exorbitant bounties of nature, away from the noise and crackle of civilization. Some of the popular routes and centres vital for trekking are as follows:

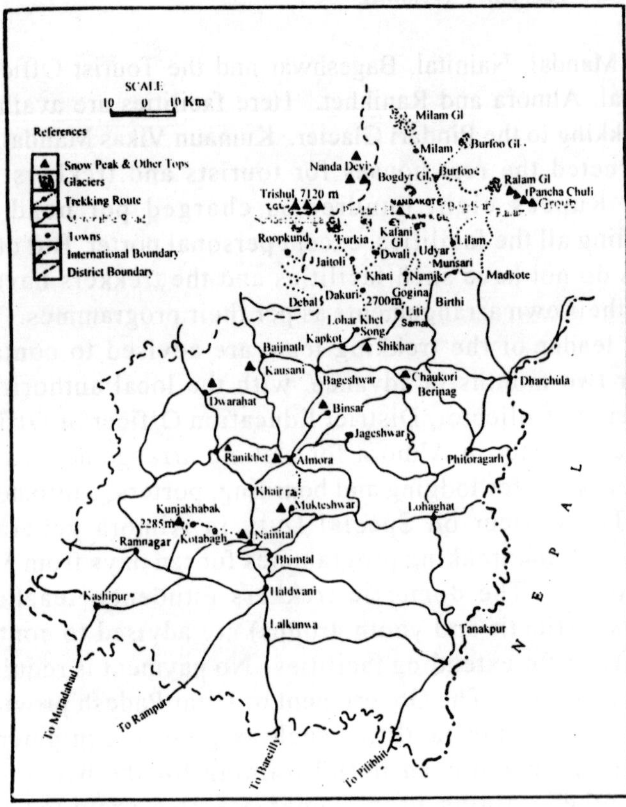

FIG. 7.1 : Trekking Resorts in Lesser Himalayan Region

Nainital

Much has been written about Nainital and adjacent areas in the earlier chapters. They however dealt with conventional tourism and the availability of facilities only. Various spots around this town provides trekking spots for the beginners, mostly one day programmes. Some of the such spots are included in Table 7.2.

Besides the above places, Hanuman Garhi known for its sun set scenery, Sat Tal, Bhimtal, Naukuchiyatal, Khurpatal and many other lesser known spots are available which cannot be used for trekking only but also for natural beauty. For example, Lands End (2118 m) is 4 km away from Nainital and provides a magnificent view of the Khurpatal plains, terraced fields, hillside and sun set.

TABLE 7.2 : Trekking spots around Nainital

Peak/Spot	Height (in metre)	Distance (in km.)
1. Naina Peak	2,610	5
2. Kilbury *	2,528	10
3. Lariya Kanta	2,481	6
4. Camels' Back	2,435	4
5. Deopatta	2,333	3
6. Dorothy's Seat	2,290	3
7. Snow View **	2,270	2

* Covered by rich natural vegetation.

** A high power Binocular has been established.

Milam Glacier

Milam is the biggest glacier of the region which is also known as the "Dream Land" of the trekkers. This famous glacier sprawls between 30^0 25' to 30^0 31' north and 79^0 50' to 80^0 east lying in the extreme north of the region at an elevation of 38,939 m and covers an area of 9 km in length and 3 km in width. It is situated in the Johar valley which was at one time the base of the Raja Zohar's Kingdom. Britishers had penetrated in these northern valleys and named these people as Bhotias in general. The people of the Johar valley have always been agriculturists, travellers and traders. Every winter they still migrate to the lower valleys. Their trade, way of life and interaction was more with the people of Tibet before the Chinese aggression in 1962. Tibet makes their northern borders. They have distinct features and their subsistence economy is based on livestock, primarily goats.

Further, Milam is a magnificent glacier with huge quantity of snow which originates from Nanda Devi (7,819 m) and other lofty mountain peaks. Trekkers have always been attracted by its beauty. It is 56 km away from Munsiary, the nearest motor head. Pithoragarh district has four camping centres, i.e. Litam, Bogadyar, Martoli or Burfoo, and Milam village. Munsiary is 321 km from Haldwani with many motorable routes, such as Tanakpur-Munsiary via Sheraghat. Generally the motor drive takes one full day journey which is much tiresome. Hence trekkers are advised to break their journeys either in Pithoragarh or Almora or Bageshwar and it will be convenient to reach Munsiary on the second day. Dak Bungalow, schools and a few hotels are available for accommodation. On reaching Munsiary, the trekker have to get their permit passes from the sub-divisional magistrate (Deputy Collector) for the Milam glacier. Two photographs are required for this purpose. Camera or binocular are not allowed. For Munsiary the trekker are advised to keep an emergency packet of lunch which may include half kilograms of fried gram, toffees, cold drinks, dry fruits, popins and glucose. The first day trekking is from Munsiary to Lilam near the bank of Gori Ganga, 11 km away from Munsiary. There is a P.W.D. rest house and the permission for its use is given from sub-divisional officer, P.W.D. Munsiary.

The second day trekking starts from Lilam to Bogdyar (2,608 m) which is 14 km away. It is only in Lilam that the permit passes will be checked by the police. From Lilam to Bodgyar, there is very rich natural vegetation but without any settlements. At Bodgyar the passes will again be verified by the police. A P.W.D. rest house and a few huts are available to take rest at night. In the third day trekking is from this place to Mirtoli or Burfoo (3,335 m) covering an area of about 21 km. At Mirtoli only a few houses are available for night stay, while at Burfoo there are many houses and a primary school available for the same purpose.

From Burfoo to Milam village (3,491 m) there is only 7 km trekking and upto the glacier only 3 km far from Milam village.

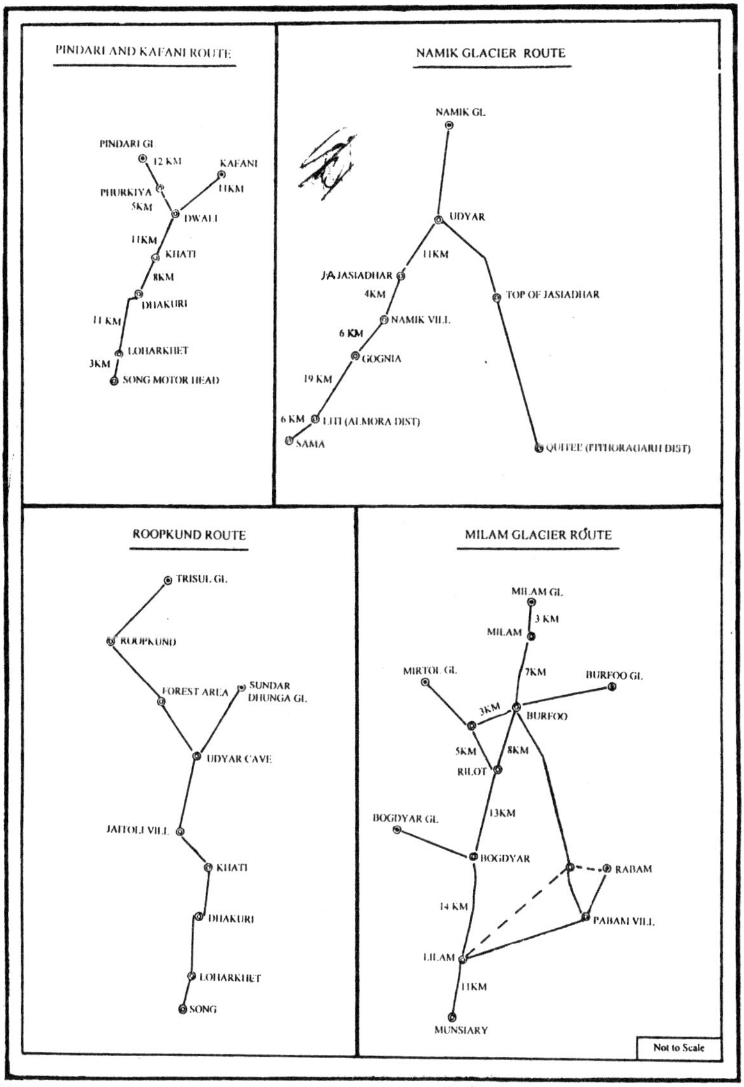

FIG. 7.2 : Route Map of Glaciers

This is the biggest village of the Johar valley. The houses, ruins, carvings on the doors and agricultural fields do indicate the past glory of the region. The whole valley was once very rich in medicinal plants. They are still found here and are commercially important. In the eight to ten days trek, one is richer by an experience unmatched elsewhere. One has to be a really litterateur to describe the beauty of the nature which is of course beyond the scope of this book.

At Milam village, a verification of all the belongings will be made by the police. There are many houses, primary school and P.W.D. rest house here for having the night stay. Next day trekking should be started in the early morning in order to take advantage of clear weather during the noon and afternoon. The weather in the night becomes cloudy and foggy. The lofty and beautiful mountains peaks can only be seen in clear weather. Further, the trekker should have enough knowledge and training for walking on the glacial moraine and snow which is extremely difficult. On the top of the mountains there are two magnificent lakes with most clear and trichocyst coloured water surrounded by coloured stones of various shapes and shades. This is a tremendous sight for the trekker. The return journey is made the same way covering a distance of 112 km in 8 to 10 days.

On the route to the Milam glacier, there are many other glaciers and spots worth seeing, e.g. Ralam, Burfoo, Mirtoli, Bodgyar, various glaciers and Mirtoli and Burfoo village temples. The Ralam glacier is also very beautiful but rather difficult to reach. The trekking starts from Lilam to Ralam village (3,507 m) which is 16 km away. From the latter village the glacier is only 13 km away. On the return journey, the trekker can reach Burfoo village which is 21 km away from Ralam village. The second glacier is Bodgyar and the third is the Mirtoli glacier. Both, can be visited from the villages by the same names. Incidentally, as per the local belief, females are not allowed for trekking to Burfoo glacier. Johar valley was once very rich but now all the fourteen villages of the Bhotiyas are merely summer centres for a few families and most of the beautiful houses have been ruined. The valley is flat and fertile.

Pindari Glacier

Pindari glacier is trekkers' paradise. It is a star attraction and magnificent glacier of the region. It lies between 30^0 16' to 30^0 23' north and 79^0 48' to 79^0 57' east in the northern part of the region stretching 3.5 km in length and 500 m in width. The elevation is 3,820 m at the mouth of the glacier. Britishers first invaded here for trekking. The rising of the sun is worth seeing. It receives huge snow form the adjacent lofty mountain peaks. This glacier, known as the "Soul of Kumaun", is about 48 km away from Song (Almora district), the nearest motor head. Night stay can be made in several centres, such as Loharkhet, Dhakuri, Khati, Dwali and Furkia. The motorable distance from Haldwani and Song is 225 km via Kausani; and 210 km via Takula. This journey takes one full day to reach Loharkhet (1,753 m above MSL). One can take the Kumaun Vikas Mandal buses or make own arrangements. The individual trekker can book various rest houses for food and lodging by paying about Rs. 800 per person. The trekking teams are advised to approach the Deputy Collector and Executive Engineer at Bageshwar to reserve dak bungalow at various places so that the lodging problem can be taken care of. Team leaders may also send a person in advance for making arrangements at Song. From Loharkhet to this place it is only 3 km distance by road, and one and half kilometres by foot. There is dak bungalow and a few houses for the night stay. On the second day, after taking breakfast, a packet lunch should be given to the trekker. It should mostly contain dry food, such as half kilogram of gram, toffees, biscuits, dry fruits and glucose etc. The route from Loharkhet to Dhakuri is rather rough. This ten kilometres steep upward route makes trekker fatigue. This journey takes at least 5 to 6 hours for an average trekker, but the bulky and weak ones will take 7 to 8 hours to reach Dhakuri (2,690 m above MSL). However, on the way there are many tea stalls. A magnificent view of the Himalaya peaks and adjacent hills is seen from this dak bungalow which is surrounded by rich natural vegetation. The third day the 8 km journey is from Dhakuri to Khati, the last village of the region towards north. It is a comfortable journey and the latter is a very beautiful village. There is a dak bungalow, tourist rest house, schools and other houses for night stay. The fourth day trekking starts from Khati (2,663 m above MSL) to Dwali to cover a distance of 12 km only. There is dak bungalow and a rest house for the night stay. On the next day trekking should start towards the magnificent Pindari glacier at about 4 a.m. so that the trekker may reach in time up to the Zero point without luggage. They should take sufficient packed lunch because at the higher elevations generally one feels very hungary. The journey is again about 12 km. but some trekkers prefer to go to Furkia for the night stay. Furkia is 5 km away from Dwali and on the route to the Zero point. The distance from Furkia to Zero point is 7 km which is very difficult to negotiate due to steep slope and ascending to high elevation. After reaching to the Zero point, the soul of Kumaun, the famous Pindari glacier can be seen, which of course is an elation and a life long ambition for a trekker.

During the month of June the trekkers can play on the snow near the Zero Point, but after this month snow is melted. Around mid-day trekkers should return from the glacier because of bad weather. On the sixth day, the trekkers, should again start at 4 a.m. for Kafani glacier which is smaller in size. This glacier in the next valley is only 10 km away from Dwali and the route is comparatively easy. Nevertheless, Kafani is more beautiful than the Pindari glacier and the one can enjoy trekking on the glacier while Pindari is rather very difficult for this purpose. The return journey should start from the next (7th) day which is easy because the trekking will be down the slope. Trekkers can even cover 19 km from Dwali to Dhakuri in one day. Besides the glaciers and natural scenery, there are numerous waterfalls throughout the route which refreshes the trekkers.

Sundar Dhunga

It is a small but very beautiful glacier at an elevation of 3,811 m. Its route starts from Khati to Jaitoli which is 11 km away and is difficult. At Jaitoli trekkers can have night stay. Further, the 13 km journey from this place to Udyar needs local guide. The trekkers are advised to take tent with them for the night stay at Udyar from where the glacier is only 9 km. This journey is also difficult due to rugged topography and a proper route is not constructed. Unlike other glaciers, the snow is quite clear at the moraine. The real nature's beauty of the glacier can be seen at Sundar Dhunga from where the return journey can be initiated.

Some of adventurous trekkers are advised to trek a new route to the Roop Kund (5,030 m above MSL), south west of Trisul (7,120 m above MSL) and Trisul glacier. The famous kund is 35 km ahead from Udyar, near Sundar Dhunga. From Roop Kund the trekkers will reach Bedal (Dhamoli) within three or four days covering a distance of nearly 54 km. This route is most fascinating and full of adventure. Besides the checklist equipments, the tents and local shepherd guide are must with the trekkers otherwise it is too dangerous to trek this new route. Sometimes the trekkers get lost. From Debal one can return to Almora.

Namik Glacier

The Namik glacier is also important and beautiful glacier of the region which gives a challenge to the adventurous trekkers because of its location, beauty and an off route glacier which sprawls over the extreme north of the region. There are two routes to cover the glacier, i.e. via Queetee (Pithoragarh), and via Sama (Almora) or Tili. The trekkers have to travel in bus upto these two points and from there the trek starts upto the magnificent glacier. The first route via Queetee to the top of the Namic village is 18 km. From this point to Udyar is 14 km and upto glacier 9 km more. The second route starts from Lite to Gogina covering a distance of 18 km which is a easy way. From this place to the Namik village top the distance is 14 km and ahead the route is same as the first one. However, from this village to the glacier the local shepherds can guide the way. No proper route exists. One will be impressed by the natural beauty consisting of various kinds of vegetation, wild animals and birds. Namik is the last village of this region and is 25 km from the glacier. Generally the hunters of this village cover this distance within one day. There is a famous site and a temple of Hunkaradevi near Namik village. The total required trekking time is 7 to 8 days. Only at Gogina there is a primary school and a few houses to have night rest, and in the remaining places trekkers have to stay in the tents or in rock Caves. Similarly, the return journey can be planned accordingly. Generally trekkers prefer to use the first route and return by the second route.

Kunj Kharak

This trekking centre is not in the glacier area. It is located 35 km away from the Nainital town and lies in the same district. The trekkers should start from Nainital to Pangot covering a distance of 9 km and then to Binayak which is 8 km more. This is an easy route. Night stay can be made in Binayak where there is a forest rest house and other houses available for accommodation. On the second day a distance of 17 km is to be covered in order to reach Kunj Kharak. One can stay here either in the forest rest house or in tents. This place is situated on the top of the Shauchalia at an elevation of 2,285 m. All arrangements should be made in Nainital as nothing is available here and there is no settlement around. The route to this place is however rich in natural vegetation. The visitor can enjoy sun rise, sun set and the natural splendour. The return journey can be alike, or the trekkers may go down to Betalghat (16 km) or Kotabagh (18 km) to get the bus.

In brief, these are a few of the places for trekking in which the authors have their own experiences. There are several other places which can be developed for trekking and tourism. From Almora, Ranikhet, Kausani and Dwarahat, numerous points are available for one day trekking for beginners.

Chapter 8

EPILOGUE

Tourism has now developed in the form of a major industry in the Nainital region which is of course a recent phenomenon. Nevertheless, the region was not unknown in the past. The early visitors were the pilgrims. They used to visit some places in the region like Ranikhet, Dwarahat and Chaukhutia on their way to better known religious shrines in Kedarnath and Badrinath. Further, many resorts owe their existence and development to the then British rulers. The British Indian Army had also a role to play in this process. But tourist influx is a recent development. Nainital is considered as an ideal tourist centre with all its limitations and advantages. The development of the other centres has direct relevance with their respective connections with this town. Some have grown as a fallout or second preference to Nainital. But, in general this town has attracted all development at the expense of the other centres of the region.

The various satellite industries linked with tourism have been benefited by tourism boom. There has been all round economic development in the region. Despite such progress, it has a long way to go to make its place in the country's tourism industry. This region has innumerable tourist attractions such as historical and archaeological monuments, religious shrines and scenic attractions lying side by side. One of the major limiting factor is the transportation. It is not served by a fast and comfortable mode of transport. A more determined effort for the planning of this region from the tourism angle is required. However, the major function of tourism planning must be to project, conserve and maximise both natural and man made environment (Kayastha, 1973). Obviously, in order to make the tourism industry profitable, the aspects of environmental pollution should not be neglected.

Development of the Tourist Centres

The place where tourists make their first stoppage is of course is Nainital, and other centres are visited from here. However, the Jim Corbett National Park is different. Considering the facilities available, three types of tourist centres can be identified :

(a) Developed,

(b) Semi developed or developing, and

(c) Potential tourist centres (Fig. 8.1).

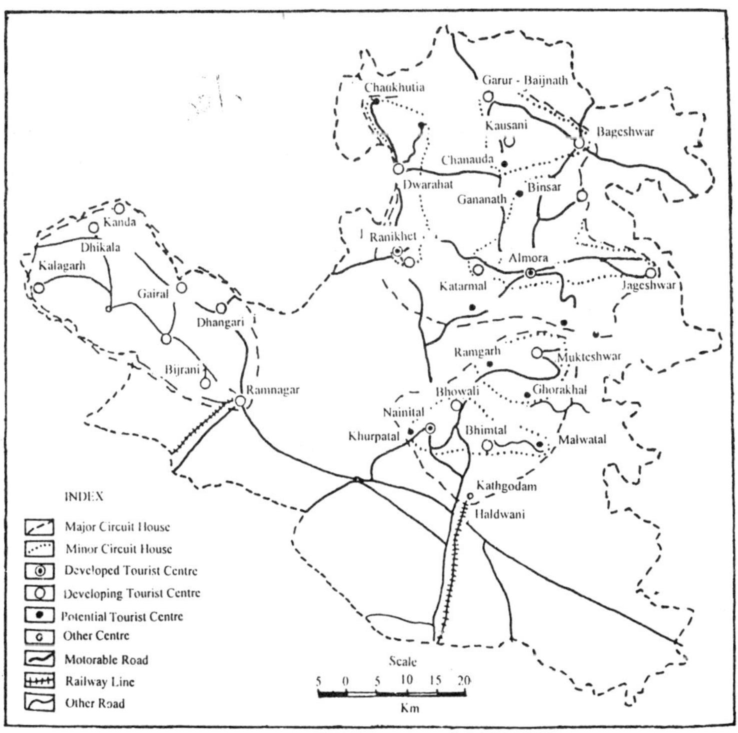

FIG. 8.1 : Nainital Region : Proposed Planning for Tourism Development

Nainital is considered as a developed tourist centre or primary centre of tourist attraction, providing almost all facilities to the visitors. Many tourists enjoy their holidays here. As a result this centre is crowded during the peak tourist seasons. On the other hand, during the lean season, such facilities are under used which create seasonal unemployment.

The official promoters of tourism, i.e. Uttar Pradesh Tourism Department and Kumaun Mandal Vikas Nigam, are trying to solve the problem of so-called peaking by diverting the tourists from Nainital to other subsidiary centres. Arrangements of package tours for the excursion by providing comfortable and cheap facilities at various spots can also help in reducing tourist pressure in Nainital.

Developing centres can be defined as secondary tourist centres of the region which are also having seasonal pressure of tourists. Priority is needed to maintain the tourist attractions and proper development of the tourist facilities in such centres.

Although, tourist complex of Nainital is almost in good condition but tourist complex of Almora comprising as a major tourist centre of the study region still needs much attention to become more popular among the tourists. The complex consists of Kausani, Ranikhet, Baijnath, and Jageshwar. Other tourist centres are Bhimtal, Mukteshwar, Bhowali and others. All these centres require to be developed as modern tourist centres. Better arrangements of transportation, boarding and lodging facilities and the development of tourist infrastructure should be provided.

Trekking routes are suffering from the problems of obscuration, viz. tourists leave filthy elements and garbage even of non-biodegradable materials like polythene bags, plastic wrappers, empty tins, bottles and waste food along the road side and in the resorts. Further, the lakes are shrinking in size due to encroachments and are being polluted with the local drainage and siltation owing to the construction of hotels. The domestic refuge, eroded debris and other waste materials are being brought to the lakes through open channels. Hence, human health may seriously be impaired and floral and faunal species can be affected. The most dwindling impact of tourism can be seen at the picnic spots, national parks and sanctuaries and other wilderness areas rather than in the resorts through the outdoor recreation activities (Wall & Wright, 1977). The associated impacts can be noticed by the increasing demand of natural resources by the tourists which may ultimately disturb the ecological balance.

The sub-committee on Ecology in a meeting of the Directors of Tourism of all the State Governments held in Mumbai concludes that the increasing number of tourists need not necessarily soil the ecology of Himalaya areas only if the flow of tourists, trekkers, mountaineers and infrastructure facilities can be controlled properly (Tyagi, 1982). For the improvement of the environmental quality at the tourist centres the restrictions should be imposed on the uncontrolled growth of dwelling constructions on the ridges to check the possibilities of landslides. In order to prevent soil erosion the fast growing plants should be planted and be protected from livestock. Alternative source of energy must be made available and frequently provided to the local residents and tourists as well. Increasing dependency upon forests and other natural sources for individual benefits in business should be stopped immediately.

Sewage discharge of the town into the lakes must be restricted or permitted to be poured in only after the required treatment in all the resort towns for keeping them clean. The work of the covered drainage and disposal of sewage technically should be started in large scale. Further, needless to say that polluted air particularly in the health resorts can distract tourists. Promotion of eco-values at government, voluntary and individual levels should be encouraged. Installation of cement or wooden benches, rain shelters, tea stalls at various spots along with small flower beds and decorative electric lights would add to the beauty of the resorts. Drinking water and toilet facilities are essential for the promotion of tourism.

Planning for the Promotion of Tourism

While interacting with the nature, the tourist would like to have new or fresh experiences different from his usual place of stay. This region has many things to offer in this regard. Nainital tourist complex is in a way a conglomeration of tourist complexes clustered around Nainital town. These secondary complexes have to be taken into account for an organic development of the whole region. Such an exercise requires proper utilization of available resources and potentialities (Fig.8.2).

These complexes consists of Nainital itself, Bhowali, Ramgarh, Mukteshwar which also covers Bhimtal, Naukuchiatal, Sat Tal and popularly known as Lake Basin District (similar to the Lake District in the U.K.). Next is the Almora tourist complex which comprises of tourists centres lying in the north of the earlier complex. It includes Almora, Ranikhet, Chaubattia, Kausani, Binsar, Katarmal and Lumgarh. It is a unique combination of historical, archaeological and natural attraction along with Jageshwar, Bageshwar, Baijnath and Dwarahat. These resorts can be developed as modern tourist centres. The Jim Corbett National Park also plays a unique role in attracting the tourists.

The resorts of the Lake Basin have been under utilized from tourism point of view. The lakes can be developed which have the potentiality to provide an additional dimension to this smokeless industry. The new attractions can be boating, fishing, swimming, yachting, bird watching, horse riding, strolling, trekking and other form of water based recreation. The pressure of tourists can certainly be reduced with the development of these resorts. However, lately, the Kumaun Mandal Vikas Nigam, Department of Tourism of Uttar Pradesh and the local authorities are taking interest in the integrated development of these resorts. Bhimtal, Sat Tal, Naukuchia Tal, Malwa Tal will soon prove to be important centres in the tourist map of India.

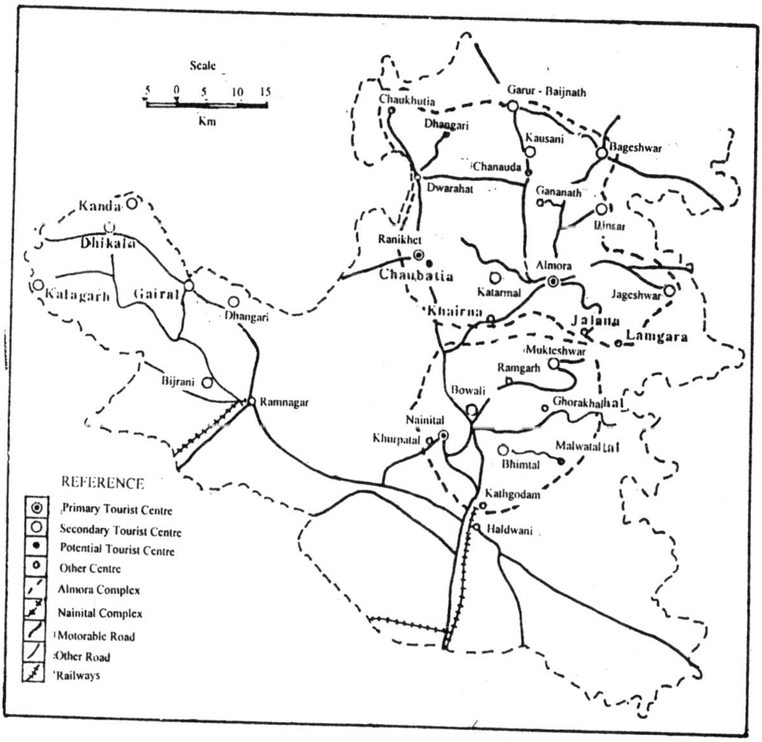

FIG. 8.2 : Nainital Region : Tourist Complexes

In several recent studies, Singh has emphasized that tourists in Nainital look for peace and want to go to places where they can avoid noisy urban environment. A tentative diffusion of tourists activity for the lake basin of Kumaun has been suggested by J. Kaur (Table 8.1). According to her, noise means a mechanical life of the metropolitan cities where a man has to work like a machine. In the Nainital region tourists feel themselves free from such mechanical life.

TABLE 8.1 : Tentative diffusion of tourist activity in the Lake Basin

Centres	Type of proposed activities	Class of tourists	Infrastructure inputs
Sat Tal	Trekking, forest rambling, perception, swimming and angling	Student, middle income group and Nainital escapees	Cottage and caravans, huts, low cost tea stalls and restaurants also at link roads
Bhimtal	Water sports, boating, surfing, swimming, orchard viewing	Foreign and high income domestic tourists	One or two star hotels, tea stalls and restaurants, recreational clubs and social entertainment centres
Naukuchiya Tal	Bird watching, boating, angling, and duck shooting and pleasure walking	Sober tourists, old group domestic and foreign tourists	Tourist Bungalow, good Indian type accommodation, boating centre.

Source : Kaur, 1980.

Visitors are interested in sober tourist activities, e.g. viewing nature, orchard and wilderness, bird watching, forest rambling, horse riding, strolling and the like. Small resorts like Mukteshwar, Ramgarh and Bhowali can provide some of the above recreations. There has to be a balance in providing the modern amenities but without disturbing the natural gifts. Excursion and one day trips can be organized in order to introduce these centres to the tourists.

A strategy for the development of tourism has to be based on different target groups so that the specific needs can be met. The requirements of pilgrims, students, trekker, middle income and high income groups are different. Perhaps to start with a new policy for the development, different resorts may be chosen for a specific group, and in the second stage these centres should cater for more than one group and finally they become multi character or cosmopolitan. Such a strategy will help the planners to concentrate their energy and resources in more concrete way. Tourist network or complexes should have a relook. The seasonal variations of the flow of tourists can be tackled to a certain extent.

One hand there are small tourists resorts which are awaiting development due to their unfavourable locations; while on the other hand, there are so-called gateway centres (Haldwani, Kathgodam and Ramnagar) which have insufficient infrastructure to meet the peak season tourists' requirements. Recently, a three star hotel has been constructed at Haldwani. Old tourists or pilgrims would like to stop here for a day or two for taking rest and getting themselves prepared for the journey to the higher altitudes.

Almora, Ranikhet and Kausani form a group of tourist resort within the region where the nature has squander its treasure of beauty with open hands. All these places need more attention for becoming much popular and the best tourist resorts. Panoramic views of the snow clad Himalayan ranges, thickly forested mountains, purely traditional habitat are the testimonial of the unfolded beauty of nature. Cottages, caravans, tourist bungalows and other types of accommodation are needed for the students, middle income group tourists, and even the high income domestic tourists. Fortunately these resorts are always preferred by the foreign tourists. In tourist season, Almora and Ranikhet are overburdened. Therefore, Kausani, Chaubattia, Lumgara and Binsar must be developed in a planned way to reduce the traffic from the major centres.

Further, there is one more group of resorts comprising of Jageshwar, Bageshwar, Baijnath and Dwarahat which are being historically and archaeologically important, apart from there natural beauty. They have the potentiality for the development as modern tourist centres. In order to achieve this objective, accommodation and other tourist facilities for various types of tourists should be made available.

Chukhutia, Dwarahat, Someshwar and Bageshwar are the valley side resorts having very limited tourist activities however still awaiting facelift. Surfing, angling, duck shooting etc. can be introduced in the river in these resorts. Tourist guest houses having capacity of atleast 50 beds and with adequate modern facilities should be constructed near the roadside.

The Nainital tourist complex as a whole needs much tourist recreational activities and facilities. A wander at the Jim Corbett National Park indicates the possible sources of disturbance to the wildlife. Obviously construction activities inside the park should be avoided to the maximum possible. However, the park is to be developed according to the international standards.

The economic benefits of trekking have been under estimated. It involves an additional set of local people to sustain the growing interest in this sport, and the advantages are not limited to the urban centres. Local people can provide food and accommodation, and become guide and porters. Local food products can be sold and tea stalls can be made on the trekking routes. The interior region is economically backwards and there are no alternative sources of employment. The promotion of trekking activities will certainly help in developing the economic condition of the region where it is most necessary.

Foregleam

In the international market of tourism, a new trend has set in. People no longer want to go to a hotel and sit beside a pool or to go to a beach and just relax. Sometimes such visits become so hectic that tourist feel more exhausted afterwards. They no longer feel refreshed. The obvious options is to visit the lesser Himalayan region. In order to cater to this new phenomenon, a very close scientific planning is required. Different agencies associated with tourism have an important role to play. The most important being the government itself as it is fully aware of the economic benefits of the additional facilities such as adventure sports or trekking. It requires a comprehensive publicity programme through television, films and magazines. The advantage of audio-visual revolutions should be taken for this purpose which is mostly government controlled.

There are definite linkages between the promotion of tourism and involvement of the local people in this industry. Healthy economic relationship has to be developed. Profiteers, and careless promoters are to be discouraged in one way or the other. Incidentally the regional economy is largely based on the tourism in this region. Fortunately, due to the problems in other places of tourist interest in the country, this region incrcasingly drawing more and more tourists. This occasion has been under utilized though the region has the potentiality to attract more and more visitors of all types. Perhaps no region in the country has attractions for pilgrims, trekker, foreign and domestic tourist from all income groups. Only determined and co-ordinated efforts are required to meet the challenge.

REFERENCES

Kaur, J. (1980), Re-evaluating Nainital Tourist : Capacity for diffusion and planned tourism activity in the Kumaun Lake Basin, in Singh, T.V. (ed), *Studies in Himalayan Ecology and Development Strategies*, The English Book Store, New Delhi, pp. 210-217.

Kayastha, S.L. (1973), The policy for the growth of tourism, editorial notes, *National Geographical Journal of India*, Vol. XI, Pt. II.

Nag, P. and Sengupta, S. (1992), *Geography of India*, Concept Publishing Company, New Delhi.

APPENDICES

Appendix I

Mean monthly temperature at different resorts in the Nainital region

(in ^{0}C)

Month	Nainital	Almora	Ranikhet	Mukteshwar	Haldwani	Ramnagar
January	6.0	7.9	7.8	5.8	13.1	20.8
February	8.7	11.2	9.6	8.1	14.1	23.9
March	12.2	14.1	13.5	11.1	21.4	29.9
April	16.7	18.1	18.4	15.4	25.4	33.9
May	19.2	21.2	19.9	18.7	30.5	38.9
June	20.5	23.9	22.1	19.0	31.9	39.7
July	18.7	22.9	20.0	17.6	30.0	35.7
August	19.2	22.5	19.5	13.3	25.4	32.4
September	18.7	22.9	19.1	17.0	26.1	31.7
October	17.6	18.5	16.1	14.2	25.0	30.4
November	14.2	16.6	13.2	11.2	19.6	27.7
December	8.3	10.6	10.1	8.2	14.0	23.3

Source : Meteorological stations at above places

Appendix II

Mean monthly distribution of rainfall at different resorts in the Nainital region
(in cm)

Month	Nainital	Almora	Ranikhet	Mukteshwar	Haldwani	Ramnagar
May	19.2	21.2	19.9	18.7	30.5	38.9
January	7.0	4.8	5.8	5.5	4.4	4.1
February	7.5	4.8	5.9	6.4	5.4	4.4
March	5.3	4.4	4.7	4.8	3.0	2.0
April	2.9	2.6	3.2	3.6	1.3	1.1
May	7.6	5.2	5.3	5.8	3.5	3.1
June	38.6	14.7	14.8	18.6	35.1	17.2
July	70.4	25.4	33.6	31.4	60.7	43.6
August	69.4	24.0	34.3	31.2	59.1	46.0
September	33.2	13.2	16.7	20.1	29.0	9.6
October	5.9	3.4	3.8	4.8	3.9	3.5
November	0.3	0.7	0.8	1.1	0.3	0.6
December	2.5	0.9	2.4	2.7	0.9	2.0

Source : Meteorological stations at above places

Appendix III

Tourism traffic in Jim Corbett National Park (1975 to 1986)

Year	Staying in Park		Not staying in Park		Total
	Indian	Foreign	Indian	Foreign	
1975-76	5,522	918	2,548	54	9,042
1976-77	6,569	760	3,165	45	10,543
1977-78	7,823	1,345	2,806	95	12,078
1978-79	6,123	921	1,938	383	9,365
1979-80	4,678	1,044	3,029	88	10,839
1980-81	9,222	1,098	–	–	10,320
1981-82	5,633	1,386	6,438	20	13,444
1982-83	16,603	1,489	–	–	18,092
1983-84	17,874	1,747	–	–	19,621
1984-85	13,452	1,557	–	–	15,009
1985-86	14,055	2,088	6,633	139	22,915

Source : Field Director Office, Project Tiger, Ramnagar, Nainital.

Appendix IV

Instructions to the Trekker by the Indian Mountain Federation

Do's and Don'ts :

(a) Trekker should not leave and throw wrappers of toffees, biscuits, cold drinks, cigarrettes and other articles on the open route. They are advised to leave these wrappers in such a place where nobody could see it, this shows the culture of the trekker. All the trekker should collect all these articles with them, after reaching at the destination all the trekker should collect it jointly and should buried in a pit, similarly they should clean the night resting place. The organizers and team leader should instruct the trekker before going on the trekking.

(b) All the team leaders or organisers are advised that they should include lectures on the Himalayan ecology and make a competition on this topic during the whole duration of the trekking camp, so that the trekker may be aware of the competitions and importance of environment. The principals are also advised to include the special lectures on the environment before going to trekking so that the students may follow the nature's rule. Special lectures in the presence of local people while at the camp should be given, so that the local people may know the value of the trees and nature.

(c) All the trekker have to give an undertaking not to damage, destroy, burn any vegetation, plant, trees and keep the mountain clean before the permission is given.

(d) The pride in local dress, customs, traditions should be instilled in the local people as there are the long-term attraction for the trekker tourists.

(e) There should be increasing use of new technology like solar heater and bio-gas for the energy needs.

(f) The trekker should encourage the local people for growing vegetables, rearing poultry, dairy and other important and useful things along the trekking routes.

Appendix V

India at a glance

Area	:	32,87,263 square km
Population	:	683, 329,097 (1981); 843,930,861 (1991)
Density of population	:	267 persons per square km
Sex ratio	:	929 females/1000 males
Growth rate	:	24.66 (1971-81) 23.50 (1981-91)
Birth rate	:	32.4 per 1000 population
Death rate	:	11.1 per 1000 population
Expectation of life at birth	:	52.5 years for males 51.1 years for females
Mean age at marriage	:	23.3 for males 18.3 for females
Extent	:	8^0 4' - 37^0 6' North 68^0 7' - 97^0 25' East (With Nicobar Islands the southern extent is 6^0 45' N) North-South : 3,214 km East-West : 2,933 km
Land frontier	:	15,200 km
Coastline	:	6,100 for mainland 5,516.6 with islands
Extent of Himalayas	:	2400 km in length 240-320 km in width
Ganga plain	:	-Do-
Languages	:	18 (as per the 8th schedule of the Constitution and subsequent modifications).
Date of Independence	:	15 August 1947
National Calendar	:	Based on Saka era with Chaitra as the first month.

Contd.

Appendix – V (*Contd.*)

National animal	:	Majestic tiger (Pavotigris)
National bird	:	Indian peacock (Pavocris-tatus)
Total road length	:	1,772 thousand km
Villages connected with all-weather roads	:	2,35,000
Railway routes	:	618,000 kilometres
Post offices	:	Urban - 15,600 Rural - 1,28,800
Telegraph offices	:	37,600
Educated manpower	:	47,724,000
Number of factories	:	96,706
Electricity generated	:	201.9 Bn. Kwh.
Villages electrified	:	4,26,323
Forest cover	:	642,000 square km
Irrigated area	:	113.3 million ha
Availability of foodgrain	:	466 grams/capita/day
All type of vehicles on road (1986)	:	10,226,000
India's share in world tourism (1986)	:	0.43 per cent

Appendix VI

Foreign Tourists visiting India

(*in '000s*)

Nationality	1971	1980	1990	1995	1996
Afganistan	6.2	10.8	20.5	10.9	12.9
Australia	10.9	22.6	30.1	36.1	48.8
Austria	1.8	7.2	10.3	13.1	17.1
Canada	7.0	23.8	41.4	63.8	74.0
France	16.8	58.7	79.5	82.3	93.3
Germany	17.9	54.7	71.4	89.0	99.9
Iran	2.8	20.9	22.7	12.3	12.2
Italy	6.0	29.0	49.2	53.0	49.9
Japan	11.6	30.6	59.1	76.0	99.0
Kenya	6.6	6.6	13.8	17.4	19.2
Malaysia	17.8	26.4	34.3	50.0	53.4
Netherland	3.7	11.2	24.4	40.1	40.2
Russia	3.5	11.0	37.7	40.7	41.1
Saudi Arabia	0.9	23.5	17.3	16.3	17.7
Singapore	7.6	16.6	32.6	48.6	47.1
Spain	1.1	11.4	18.6	24.4	24.4
Sri Lanka	16.6	68.4	68.4	114.2	107.4
Sweden	2.8	7.1	13.3	19.0	21.2
Switzerland	5.4	13.3	32.4	29.4	35.0
Thailand	3.4	10.9	11.9	14.5	16.2
U.K.	40.4	102.5	235.2	334.8	360.7
U.S.A.	55.0	78.6	125.3	203.3	228.9
TOTAL (Including others)	301.0*	800.2*	1,707.2	2,123.7	2,287.9
Foreign Exchange Earning (Rs. Crore)	45.0	1.166.0	2,444.0	8,640.0	10,061.4

* Excluding Bangladesh and Pakistan.

Source : *Statistical Outline of India*, Tata Services Limited, Mumbai, 1998.

BIBLIOGRAPHY

Atkinson, E.T. (1974), *Kumaun Hills,* Cosmos Publication, Delhi (reprinted).

Arora, K.K. (1971), Tourist Industry in Kumaun, Ph. D. thesis, Agra University, Agra (unpublished).

Anand, M.M. (1976), *Tourism and Hotel Industry In India–A study in Management,* Printice Hall of India Pvt. Ltd., New Delhi.

Asthana, V.K. (1968), Landforms and Settlement in Almora and its Environs, Ph.D. thesis, Banaras Hindu University, Varanasi (unpublished).

Bisht, D.S.(1982), *Guide to Garhwal and Kumaun Hills*, Trishul Publication, Dehra Dun.

Binani, G.D. and Rama Rao, T.V. (eds) (1953), *India at a Glance: A Comprehensive Reference Book of India*, Orient Longmans Ltd., Calcutta.

Boesch, H. (1964), *A Geography of World Economy,* D. van Nostrand Co.

Caleb, B.E. (1971-72), *The Kumaun Hills and U.P. Hill Stations,* Moradabad Printing Works, Moradabad.

Cunnigham, A., Archaeological Survey of India Report, Vol XIV.

Cosgrove, I. and Jackson, R. (1972), *The Geography of Recreation and Leisure* Hutchinson University Library, London.

Clawson, M. (1971), *Recreational Resource in Conservation of Natural Resources*, John, Wiley & Sons, New York.

Dattar, B.N. (1961), *Himalayan Pilgrimage*, Publication Division, New Delhi.

Department of Tourism (1982), *Tourism Statistics*, Government of India, New Delhi.

Ferrario, F.F. (1979), The evaluation of tourist resources : An applied methodology, *Journal of Travel Research,* Vol. XVII, No. 3, Boulder.

Fonia, K.S. (1977), *Uttarakhand : Garhwal Himalaya,* Asian Journals, Dehra Dun.

Ganssar, A. (1964), *Geology of Himalayas*, Inter Science Publishers, London.

Gearing, Charles, E. *et al.* (1974), Establishing a measure of touristic attractions, *Journal of Travel Research*, Vol. XII, No. IV, University of Colorado, Boulder.

Gearing, Charles, E. *et al.* (1976), *Planning for Tourism Development : Quantitative Approaches*, Praeger, New York.

Government Press (1928), *Nainital–A Historical and Descriptive Account*, Allahabad.

Gupta, P.N. & A.K. Roy (eds) (1983), *Himalayas : Mountain Resources Management and Remote Sensing,* Surya Publication, DehraDun.

Gupta, P.N. and A.K. Roy (eds) (1991), *Mountain Resources Management and Remote Sensing,* Surya Publications, Dehra Dun.

I.U.O.T.O., (1970). *Economic Review of World Tourism*, Geneva.

Jafari, J. (1979), The tourism market–basket of goods and service The components and natue of tourism in *Tourism Recreation Research*, Centre for Tourism Research, Lucknow, Vol. IV, Pt. 1, No. 4.

Jha, M. (ed) (1985), *Dimensions of Pilgrimage*, Inter-India Publication, New Delhi.

Joshi, S.C. *et al.* (1983),*Kumaun Himalaya–A Geographical Perspective on Resource Development*, Gyanodaya Prakashan, Nainital.

Kandari, O.P. and Singh, T.V. (1982), Corbett National Park : India, in Singh, T.V., Kaur, J. and Singh, D.P. (eds), *Studies in Wildlife Parks Conservation,* Metropolitan Book Co., New Delhi.

Kaur, J. (1980), Re-evaluating Nainital tourism capacity for diffusion, planned tourism activity in the Kumaun Lake Basins, Singh, T.V. (ed), *Himalayan Ecology and Development Strategies,* English Book Store, New Delhi.

Kaur, J. (1982), Pilgrims progress to Himalayan shrines : Studying the phenomenon of religious tourism, in Singh, T.V., Kaur, J. and D.P. Singh (eds), *Tourism and Wildlife Parks Conservation,* Metropolitan Books Co. Pvt. Ltd., New Delhi.

Kaur, J. (1982), Tourism and Pilgrimage in Eastern Garhwal Himalayas–Study in Recreational and Religious Geography, Ph.D. thesis, Garhwal University, Srinagar (unpublished).

Kaur, J. (1985), *Himalayan Piligrimages and the New Tourism*, Himalayan Books, New Delhi.

Kayastha, S.L. (1973), Policy for growth of tourism, editorial notes, *National Geographical Journal of India,* Vol. XIC, Pt. II.

Kayastha, S.L. and Rai, H.C. (1983), Nainital : a case study in tourism, *Hill Geographer,* Vol. 2, No. 2.

Kayastha, S.L. (1975), *Tourism*, in Walter Imber & Hans Boesch (eds), *India*, Kummerly & Frcy, Berne.

Kayastha, S.L. (1997), Tourism and environment in the Himalayan region, in P. Nag, V. K. Kumra & J. Singh (eds), *Geography and Environment : Regional Issues*, Concept Publishing Company, New Delhi, pp. 31-45.

Kharakwal, S.C. (1969), *Landforms and Settlements in Nainital and its Environs*, Ph.D. thesis, Department of Geography, B.H.U., Varanasi.

Kharakwal, S.C. (1997), Changing environmental conditions in Himalayan and their regeneration, in P. Nag, V. K. Kumra & J. Singh (eds), *Geography and Environment : National Issues,* Concept Publishing Company, New Delhi, pp. 149-61.

Krishnan, M.S.(1960), *Geology of India and Burma*, Higginbotham's Pvt. Ltd., Madras.

Kumar, S.M. (1985), Conservation and Corbett National Park, *Yojana*, 1-15 June.

Lall, J. S. & A. D. Modie (eds) (1981), *The Himalaya : Aspects of Change*, Oxford University Press, New Delhi.

Lamba, B.S. (1977), Fauna of Corbett National Park, Cheetal, *Journal of Wildlife Society of India,* Vol. 18 (20).

Majumdar, R.C., Ray Chaudhuri, H.C. and Dutta, K. (1967), *An Advanced History of India*, Macmillan & Co., London.

Nag, P. and Sengupta, S. (1992), *Geography of India,* Concept Publishing Company, New Delhi.

Nautiyal, S.N. (1974), *Garhwal Ke Lok Nritya,* Amrit Prakashan, Ghaziabad.

Negi, J.S.M. (1982), *Tourism and Hoteliering–A Worldwide Industry,* Gitanjali Publishing House, New Delhi.

Negi, J.S. (1958), *Prayatan ka Swarg*, Bharatwasi Prakashan, Allahabad (in Hindi)

Nevilli, H.R. (ed) (1904), *District Gazetteer : Nainital*, Vols. I, XXXIV and XXXV.

N.A.T.M.O.(1985), *Glimpses of India,* National Atlas & Thematic Mapping Organisation, Calcutta.

N.A.T.M.O. (1988), *Tourist Atlas of India,* National Atlas and Thematic Mapping Organisation, Calcutta, (2nd ed).

Pande, B.D. (1936), *Kumaun ka Itihas*, Almora Shakti Press, Almora (in Hindi).

Pande, T. (1979), *Kumaun ka Lok Sahitya ki Prasth Bhumi*, Sahitya Bhavan (Pvt.) Ltd., Allahabad (in Hindi).

Pandey, T. (1962), *Kamaun ka Lok Sahitya*, Almora Book Depot, Almora (in Hindi).

Pant, P.C. (1976), Plants of Corbett National Park, Uttar Pradesh, *Journal of Bombay Natural Historical Society,* Vol. 73 (20).

Ramford, C.G. and Robinson, H. (1978), *The Geography of Transport*, MacDonald and Evans, London.

Robinson, H. (1976), *A Geography of Tourism,* Mac Donald and Evans Ltd., London.

Rawat, U.S. (1956), *Uttarakhand ki Ek Jhanki,* Lansdown (in Hindi).

Sanskrityayan,R. (1936), *Himalaya Parichaya,Kumaun,* Part(II), Law Journal Press, Allahabad (in Hindi).

Singh, C.B.(1979), *Corbett Park Tiger Reserve,* Position paper, International Symposium on Tiger, New Delhi, Feb. 22-24.

Singh, J.S. (ed) (1985), *Environmental Regeneration in Himalaya*, Central Himalayan Environmental Association, Nainital.

Singh, J.S., Singh, S.P. and Shastri, C. (eds) (1981), *Science and Rural Development in Mountains,* Gyanodaya Prakashan, Nainital.

Singh, J.S. and Singh, S.P.(eds) (1984), *An Integrated Ecological Study of Eastern Kumaun Himalaya with Emphasis on Natural Resources*, Department of Botany, Kumaun University, Nainital.

Singh, H.H., Nag, P., Kumra, V.K., Singh, S.K.,Singh, J.and Prasad, H.(eds) (1986), *Geography and Environment: Issues and Challenges*, Concept Publishing Company, New Delhi.

Singh, S.K. and Savita Singh (1997), Environmental Degradation in Uttarakhand Himalaya, in P. Nag, V.K. Kumra and J. Singh (eds.), *Geography and Environment : National Issues*, Concept Publishing Company, New Delhi, pp. 203-205.

Singh, S.P., Pant, M.C., Sharma, 1A.P., Sharma, P.C. and Purohit, R.(1982), Limnology of shallow water zones of lakes in Kumaun Himalayas (India), in Gopal, B.; Turner, R.E.; Wetzer, R.G. and Whingham, D.F. (eds), *Proceedings of Wetlands : Ecology and Management*, International Science Publishers, Jaipur, 39-40.

Singh, T.V.(1975), *Tourism and Tourist Industry in U.P.*, New Heights, New Delhi.

Singh, T.V.(1977), Prospects for Tourism Promotion in U.P. Himalaya, *Uttarakhand Bharti,* Vol. 1, No, 4, Kumaun University, Nainital.

Singh, Tejvir (1977), *The Himalayas*, Srinagar, Garhwal.

Singh, T.V. *et al.* (eds) (1982), *Studies in Tourism Wildlife Park Conservation,* Metropolitan Book Co. Pvt. Ltd., New Delhi.

Singh, T.V. and Kandari, O.P. (1980), *Corbett National Park : Studying Impact of Tourism on Developmental Activities*, Tourism and Recreational Research, Lucknow.

Singh, T.J. & J. Kaur (eds) (1983), *Himalayas : Mountain and Men*, Printhouse (India), Lucknow.

Singh, T.V., Kaur, J. and Singh, D.P. (1982), *Studies in Tourism, Wildlife Parks Conservation*, Metropolitan Book Company Ltd., New Delhi.

T.C.S. (1998), *Statistical Outline of India,* Tata Consultancy Services, Mumbai.

Tyagi, N. (1982), A geographical Study of Hill Resorts in U.P. Himalaya, Ph.D. thesis, Gorakhpur University, Gorakhpur (unpublished).

Upadhyaya,U.D.(1979), *Kumaun ki Lok Gathaon ka Sahityak aur Sanskritik Adhyayan,* Prakash Book Depot, Bareilly.

Vaishnava, Y.D. (1983), *Land and People, Himalayan District of Uttar Pradesh,* Shree Almora Book Depot, Almora.

Wadis, D.N.(1966), *Geology of India,* MacMillian & Co. Ltd., London.

Wahab, S. (1975), *Tourism Development*, Tourist International Press, London.

World Council of Churches (1970), *Leisure-Tourism : Threat and Promise,* Geneva.

Young-George (1973), *Tourism : Blessing or Blight*?, Penguin Books Ltd., Middlesex.

INDEX

Accommodation, facilities, 98, 102, 118-110; preference of, 130-31
Adventure tourism, types of, 145-46
Age-Sex structure, 125-26
Almora, 22, 55; tourist places, 55-59
Anashakta Yoga, 72
Architectural centres, 58
Atan, 17
Atkinson, E.T., 43,116
Badrinath, 19, 158
Bageshwar, 43, 83
Baijnath, 43, pilgrimage centre, 82-83; temple complex, 80
Bangladesh, 45
Banj-Oak forests, 36
Basanta Deva, 43
Bhabar tarai region, 29-30, 45
Bhairavnath temple, 83
Bhimtal, 22, 164; tourist places, 77-78
Bhotiyas, 152
Bhowali, 78; fruit market, 78
Burfoo glacier, 152
Burrard, S.G., 29
Camp equipment, 142; centres, 150
Champawat, 43
Chand dynasty, 55
Chaukhutia, 158
Chinese aggression, 149
Christian Mission, 58
Civil amenities, 102-108
Clothing and equipments, 139-40
Cold weather season, 39-40
Communication, 99, 102
Cultural dimension, 88; tourism, 95
Cyclones, 21
Dattarnath temple, 83
Deoban-Tejam zone, 29
Deshatan, 17
Dharma, 90
Dharmashalas, 109, 130
Domestic tourists, 119-23; percentage of, 127
Dwarahat, 43,158
Dwarika, 20
Economic impact, 97-98
Educational facilities, 113-14
Electricity, 110-112
Employment, 91, 131
Environmental pollution, 89
Expenditure, 99
Fair and festivals, 88-89, 92
Fayahuyan, 19
First World War, 20
Foregleam, 166-67
Foreign tourist, visiting India, 176; percentage of, 127
Gandhiji, 72, 73
Garhwal, 27
Garur-Baijnath valley, 80
Ghughitia, 92
Gita, 72
Gitanjali, 85
Golla Dewata, 97
Gori Ganga, 139
Gorkhas, 43
Gurudwaras, 94
Haily, Malcolm, 62
Haldwani, 22
Haryana, 21
Hastinapur, 79
Hot Weather Season, 41-42
Huentsang, 19
Income and expenditure, 131-43
Indian Mountain Federation, instruction to trekkers, 172-73
Indian Veterinary Research Institute (IVRI), 85
International tourists, 19-20
International Union of Official Travel Organisation, 18
Itsing, 19
Iventsiang, 19
Jagar, 97
Jageshwar,43
Jajmani system, 90
Jim Corbett National Park, 22, 27, 62, 99, 134, 137, 159,162; accommodation of 65-66; climate condition, 62-64; tourism traffic in, 171; wildlife, visibility of, 64
Johar Valley, 149,151
Joshi, S.C., 29,30
Kafani glacier, 154
Kaladhungi, 49
Karma, 90
Karti-Keyapura (Baijnath-Garur) Valley, 42
Kashipur, 22, 86
Kathgodam, 52
Kaur, J., 163
Kausani, 22, 72; tourist places, 72, 76, 112
Kaushik Muni, 72
Kayastha, S.L., 158
Kedarnath, 158
Kharakwal, S.C., 30
Khatima, 22, 26,
krol-belt, 27, 29
Kumaun, 24, 26, 55
Kumaun Vikas Mandal Nigam, 135, 145, 147, 153, 160, 162
Kunj Khorak, 156
Lake Bain district, 162
Landslides, 161
Lesser Himalaya, 30

Lloyd, P.J., 18
Longstall, T.G., 21
Lord Bagnath (Shiva), 83
Mahadevi Verma, 85
Malwa Tal, 163
Mansarovar, 17
Maths, 19
Medical facilities, 114-15
Metalled road, distribution of, 105-107
Milam glacier, 149-150, 152
Military Engineering Services (MES), 112
Minerals, 29
Moksha, 90
Motivational aspects, 133-34
Mukteshwar, 33, 85
Musical festivals, 92
Nag, P., 98
Naina Devi, 23, 49
Nainital region, 22, 25; accommodation problems, 22; civic amenities, 102-120; climate, 36-37; cultural aspects, 92-93; electricity, 110-12; lakes, 32-33; location of, 26-27; monthly temperature, 169-70; nature of tourism, 21-22; public utility services, 102-118; physical division, 28; recreational activities 23-24; socio-cultural interest, 89; trekking aspects, 149-50; transport system, 102-112; tourist complexes, 160-63; vegetation, 34-36
Nalanda University, 19
Namik glacier, 155-56
Nandadevi, 58; fair, 92
Narayan Swami, 85
Naukuchic Tal, 163
Nautyal, K.P. 42
Okhal Kanda, 27
Orchards, 80
Orography, 29
Package tour programme, 128
Pakistan, 45
Parayatan, 17
Patliputra, 128
Peters, M., 95
Physical and mental fitness, 139-40
Pindari glacier, 83, 147, 155-56
Pithoragarh, 22, 23, 43, 55
Pondicherry Ashram, 85
Purpose of visit, 119-20, 123-24
Punjab, 21
Puri, 19
Queetee (Pithoragarh), 155
Rainy season, 41
Raja Laxmi Chand, 83
Rajasthan, 21
Ramakrishna Mission, 58
Rameshwaram, 19
Ramganga National Park, 62
Ramgarh, 83
Ranikhet, 22, 58, 67, 158; cantonment, 68; forests, 70; tourist places, 70-71
Ratnagiri, 19
Ravindranath Tagore, 85
Resorts, 164, 165, 166
Retreating monsoon season, 42
Robinson, H., 91
Rudrapur, 23, 26, 86
Rural water supply scheme, 112
Sanchi, 19
Sarnath, 19
Sat Tal, 163
Satellite industries, 158
Second World War, 20
Sewage and Drainage, 30-31,113-14, 161
Shishupalgarh, 19
Siwalik, 30
Skanda Purana, 49
Sober tourist activities, 164
Species, 35
Sub-tropical diciduous forests, 35-36
Sundar Dhunga, 155
Takshashila University, 19
Tirthatan, 17
Tourist, categories of, 120-21; facilities, 108-109; income groups, 133; interest places, 48-80; guides and operators, 115; modes of travel, 128-29; occupations, 121; purpose of visits, 123-24; reactions of, 134-35; resorts, 164-66
Tourist centres; classification of, 44-45; development of, 159-60; origin of, 42-43
Tourism, elements of, 18; international market, 166; planning for promotion, 162-63
Tourism of culture, impact of, 95-96
Transportation, 23, 99, 102
Trekkers, checklist for 142-43
Trekking, economic benefits of, 166-67; facilities for, 137; glacier and non-glacier, 146; map, 145; preparations, 146-47; programme, 138-139, 142; routes and places, 147-48, 160; season, 145-46
Tripathi, S., 90
Tririshi Sarovara, 49
Trishul glacier, 155
Tyagi, N., 161
Ujjain, 19
Unemployment, 160
Uttar Pradesh, 21, 23, 42
Uttar Pradesh State Roadways Transport Corporation (UPSRTC), 107
Uttarakhand, 19
Uttarnarayani, 92; fair, 83
Vairot, 19
Wadia, D.N., 29
Waheb, S., 18
Wall, G.,18
Water Supply, 111-12
World Council of Churches, 95